More for Less

Most leadership assumptions are based on a deterministic view of the world. If you do X you should get Y, process can be employed for most things, and more complicated problems can be analysed to enable better decisions. Whilst these approaches suit the Simple and the Complicated, they do not work so well for the Complex. The Complex needs a different approach, the core of which is to enable the organisation being led to be agile and self-organising.

More for Less introduces a new paradigm for leadership, Leadership 4.0. Based on his previous book, *Complex Adaptive Leadership*, Nick Obolensky has created a simple and step-by-step approach to Leadership 4.0 whilst challenging and questioning the reader to be more effective and less busy.

This book is an essential tool for the busy leader and manager and will appeal to practitioners wishing to improve their leadership effectiveness. It will also appeal to students and researchers in the field of leadership.

Nick Obolensky has had a varied career in leadership including being a British Army Major, an Executive Consultant in Ernst & Young, a FTSE 100 Associate Director, CEO of various start ups, and visiting professor of leadership in various blue chip business schools. He has authored other books, including *Complex Adaptive Leadership*.

More for Less

The Complex Adaptive Leader

How to lead an adaptive, agile and
self-organising organisation

Nick Obolensky

Routledge
Taylor & Francis Group

LONDON AND NEW YORK

First published 2019
by Routledge
2 Park Square, Milton Park, Abingdon, Oxon OX14 4RN

and by Routledge
711 Third Avenue, New York, NY 10017

Routledge is an imprint of the Taylor & Francis Group, an informa business

British Library Cataloguing-in-Publication Data
A catalogue record for this book is available from the British Library

Library of Congress Cataloging-in-Publication Data
A catalog record has been requested for this book

ISBN: 978-1-138-06371-6 (hbk)
ISBN: 978-1-138-06372-3 (pbk)
ISBN: 978-1-315-16084-9 (ebk)

Typeset in Stone Serif
by Swales & Willis Ltd, Exeter, Devon, UK

Contents

Figures

Foreword

So what's this all about?

This book is based on the earlier best-seller book *Complex Adaptive Leadership: Embracing Paradox and Uncertainty* (recently translated into Chinese). For those too "busy" to read such a tome, this book gives the key essence. It shows how an application to leadership and/or management (an out-of-date distinction but we are where we are) of a new and powerful science, complexity science, can get better results, faster, for less effort and resource. This book asks a lot of questions, and only answers some of them – it will challenge you to come up with your own answers.

And for those wishing to dive deeper, as well as get a better understanding of the science behind the approach, the earlier book will serve as a basis for further exploration. But this assumes you:

1 Are too busy to read business books (who does?). This one is easier and even might change your mindset about what leadership is!
2 Get too many emails and too much information, and sometimes are feeling swamped . . .
3 Have a sneaky suspicion that there might just be a better way to get things done, as you often feel too busy, like a hamster on a wheel going nowhere fast . . .

Your organisation probably has a strategy. But what about you? Do you have a clear leadership strategy? We are not talking about merely implementing some strategy designed by the suits upstairs. We're talking here about the HOW you get things done, not the WHAT. This small book can set you on a path that can help you get better results, faster for less effort and stress. This means, for example:

1   Your team becomes engaged, agile and creative;
2   You can focus on important things and get off the hamster wheel;
3   You are not drowned by emails (or anything else at work for that matter);
4   You take your full holidays, uninterrupted and optimise work/life balance (a term which should be banned/met with disdain – as discussed later).

Too good to be true? Maybe it is. But on the other hand . . . what have you got to lose but possibly the chains of out-of-date assumptions that might be driving and enslaving you? And for those worried about the cost of the book or the time to digest it: if you do the exercises in this book, reflect fully on the questions asked, and then work to implement the ideas which emerge supported by regular reflective practice, and do not get value, then I personally will refund you (howzat for a guarantee?).

Nick Obolensky
Shanghai and Lille, 2018

1 *WHY leadership needs to change*

You have probably heard of the "buzzword de jour" – VUCA (Volatile, Uncertain, Complex, Ambiguous). This is seen as a problem – but it is what is (and, as you might come to see with a new mindset and understanding of the underlying science, it can be pretty amazingly cool). If you see VUCA as a problem – it is not. You are.

"Who me?" I hear you protest.

Yes you! Forgive the direct approach (but you are busy after all, so let's not beat around the bush).

So why is this? Look at the graph in Figure 1.1 below. It shows the pace of change over 4,000 years (a relatively short period of time for us as a species) against the assumptions we have held about leadership.

Notice anything? As far as the pace of change is concerned, well, this amount of change in such a short period of time (for us as a species) could be termed anthropological shock. So, if you are stressed, overwhelmed, too busy etc. – relax – this has nothing to do with you, your organisation, your industry, your country – welcome to Planet Earth. What you need is simply another way of looking at things – change how you see the world and the world will change for you. By the end of this book hopefully you will have another, more helpful, perspective.

As for leadership – seems we are a bit stuck. At any one time in the Egyptian kingdom there was one pharaoh; at any one time in a Greek city one mayor; at any one time in the Roman empire there was one emperor (OK so Caligula had two – his horse – and initially there was a republic but you get the general gist); at any

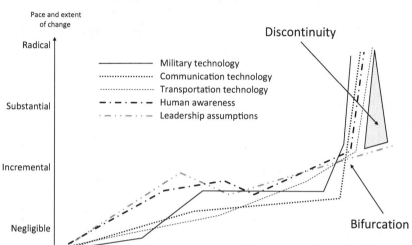

Figure 1.1 Stuck assumptions

one time in a kingdom in Europe, one king . . . and today, how many CEOs does your organisation have? Probably just one. In other words, we have changed the CONTEXT of leadership far, far faster than we can possibly change our ASSUMPTION of what leadership is. And that assumption is still pretty much what we call Leadership 1.0 – leadership slides downhill.

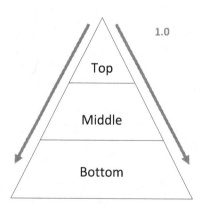

Figure 1.2 Leadership 1.0

The people at the top – we call them leaders. And those in the middle – we call them managers. Which gives a great debate on the difference between leaders and managers. And the rest? What do we call them? Lots of things, but the important ones HR calls "talent" (as the rest are clearly untalented?). And we can surround ourselves in the comforting blanket of talent pipelines, competency models etc. so we can "manage" leadership and the development of leaders. Nothing wrong. Been around a long time. And we have, after all, kept up with the times and changed our view of leadership 1.0. We have frequently redefined leadership: from the heroic "great man" leader of 170 years ago (à la Thomas Carlyle), to the decisive directive leader of 130 years ago (à la Frederick Taylor) to the transformational leader of 90 years ago (à la Mary Follet), built on and added with the transactional leader of 50 years ago (à la James Burns), to the servant leader of 40 years ago (à la Robert Greenleaf), to the empowering leader of 30 years ago (a la Julian Rappaport), to the restorative and resilient leader of 20 years ago (à la Seana Steffen), to the agile leader of 10 years ago (à la Iacocca and Witney) . . . to name but a few! However, it's all still mostly Leadership 1.0. In fact, it is *"leaders"* (good ones) that have been redefined and not so much *"leadership"* (which assumes is done by leaders). Still relevant – but by far no means longer sufficient . . . This may explain why we are struggling with VUCA – we are applying an old 1.0 paradigm to new problems . . .

Figure 1.3 VUCA
Source: Magee (1998)

- Visionary and charismatic instead of command and control
- Exercise power in a responsible way
- Invoked loyalty, faith and belief in followers
- Knows how to deal with the problems and forms winning strategies
- Has great charisma and invokes admiration – celeb status....

.....is the leadership we LIKE and WANT
the leadership we NEED?

Figure 1.4 What we like might not be what we need?

VUCA first appeared in the military – not surprising given the asymmetric warfare we seem to be engaged in – but the term is gaining frequent use in business. And a whole plethora of consultants offer ways to overcome VUCA. Sadly, most of those who offer advice still have a 1.0 mindset based on the wrong science . . . but more of that later . . . meanwhile let's get back to leadership.

Leadership has moved (for most) from the good old command and control days to a more "visionary" "transformational" leadership.

When things get messy, uncertain and unpredictable we like to look up and see clear knowledgeable leaders who we can trust, who have a clear vision with a bit of personality/charisma, who know the answers to the problems we face, who can hold power and exercise it in a positive way . . . this is certainly the leadership we like . . . the one we crave for in uncertain times . . . solid Leadership 1.0 . . . but is this what we need?

Here are some quotations, "weak signals", that something might be up, showing traditional and popular views of Leadership 1.0 may be under increasing strain:

"Subordinates need to challenge in order to follow, and superiors must listen in order to lead" (Hirschhorn and Gilmore, 1992) – so is this bye bye trust –don't trust them, challenge them?

"A charismatic visionary leader is absolutely not required for a visionary company, and in fact can be detrimental" (Collins and Porras, 1997) – bye bye charisma?

"Leading from Good to Great does not mean coming up with the answers" (Collins, 2001) – bye bye knowledgeable leaders with MBAs?

"The more power you give a single individual in the face of complexity and uncertainty, the more likely it is that bad decisions will be made" (Surowiecki, 2004) – bye bye powerful leaders?

"Complexity science shows how the typical focus on 'heroic' and charismatic leaders can result in a lack of innovation in modern organisations" (Hazy et al., 2007) – bye bye heroes and charisma (again)?

"The dominant view of leadership is that the leader has the vision and the rest is a sales problem. I think that notion of leadership is bankrupt" (Heifitz, 2013) – bye bye visionary leaders?

Now to be fair, these researchers were looking at big companies – if you are a small company with a visionary, entrepreneurial, trusted, heroic etc. leader . . . that's OK. But soon may come the time, when the company grows, that leadership will need to move from 1.0 (however defined). But towards what?

Let's see what is actually happening in big companies. They are moving from the traditional functionally divided, hierarchically sliced, to more matrixed organisations.

Interesting . . . organisations are becoming more complex to deal with a more complex world . . . so simplification is not the answer! Complexification is . . . which we explore later.

So now we need leadership not just going downwards, but also sideways and outwards. HR call this, with a 1.0 mindset, "Influencing without power". We call it Leadership 2.0. And if you are in a matrix (a 2.0 reality) with a 1.0 mindset, you are going to struggle.

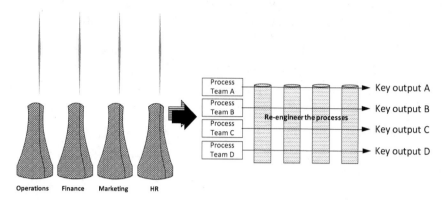

Figure 1.5 Moving to the matrix

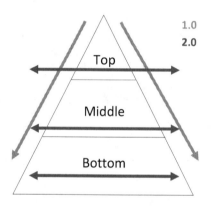

Figure 1.6 Leadership 2.0

Such an organisation means information flows sideways as well – which increases the amount of information . . . and we struggle to keep on top of it all. We feel that if we want to deal with a VUCA world, we need to keep on top of things and know everything that's going on . . . which is largely a complete waste of time as we will see later. For now look at the chart below in Figure 1.7.

It's a little out of date – but you get the idea. Of 100% of knowledge in 1990, only 10% existed in 1900 (and that number would be now be naught-point-something-pretty-low % due to the internet). And yet the more we know, the more volatile things are. But "Correlation is not causation!" I hear

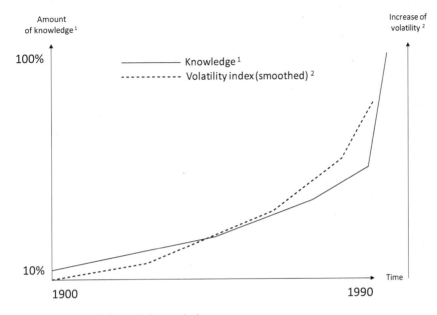

Figure 1.7 Knowledge might not help

Source: Wilton (1990); and Bradford and Grossman (1993).

Note:
1 Amount of knowledge based on Wharton/Fortune study, indexed at 100% at 1990.
2 Volatility increase, indexed at 100% at 1990.

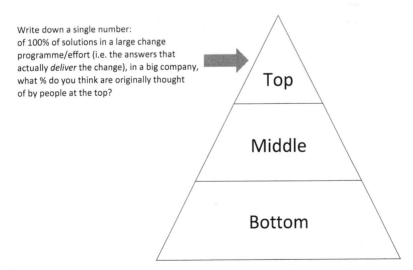

Figure 1.8 What solutions come from the top?

you cry! But in this case, it is connected – we now are more interconnected than ever before and ripple effects/unforeseen consequences abound.

So many have a 1.0 mindset in a 2.0 reality which causes stress. But it does not stop there. See figure 1.8 for a thought experiment.

What was your number? If it is over 50% then that would suggest that, more or less, you reckon that leaders know the answers to the problems . . . but you would be in a minority with that viewpoint. In reality the number is less than 20% (see the research in my book *Complex Adaptive Leadership*).

In other words, leaders no longer know. And they know they do not know . . . pretty stressful. In the old days they turned to God, today they turn to McKinsey. But they cannot say they do not know because they are expected to know . . . by everyone else, who, for the most part, know that leaders do not know anyway! This is happening all over the world. We really do want leaders to give us certainty and look upwards for it, but we know, deep down, they do not, for the most part, have the answers.

Sadly, with our 1.0 mindset we find it hard to think of any other way out of this charade . . . so leaders often pretend to know, and followers pretend not to know. Very rarely do leaders stand up and say: "I don't know". I mean, when was the last shareholder Annual General Meeting you went to when the CEO stood up and said "Beats me guys . . . any suggestions?"! The real challenge for leaders today is not only leading when they know, but also being able to lead confidentially and credibly when they do not know, enabling those who do know to take the initiative.

What we need is solutions coming upwards (HR folks call this "bottom up" change or "empowerment") but we call it leadership 3.0 . . . leading upwards. Leaders need to learn to follow those they lead, followers need to learn to lead those they follow – a paradox and conundrum. But if an organisation is to become agile, empowered, adaptive and fast moving we need effective 3.0 as part of the mix. How to do this is dealt with later.

So, if you have a 1.0 mindset in a 2.0 reality with an increasing 3.0 imperative . . . you are going to be very busy and very stressed.

Some organisations are evolving in form to match this 3.0 imperative, moving beyond the 2.0 matrix towards a fluid

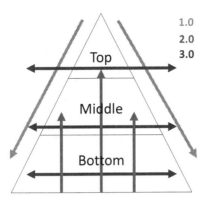

Figure 1.9 Leadership 3.0

networked organisation where teams form, deliver, disband, reform . . .

Example organisations that show this evolution include Morning Star (a tomato juice company in USA), St Luke's (an advertising company in the UK), Oticon (a hearing aid company in Denmark), Askona (a furniture company in Russia), Haier (a white goods company in China), Atlassian (a software company in Australia) . . . it's beginning to slowly emerge all over the world.

So, if you are stressed trying to get answers to "wicked problems" and feel guilty you do not know the answers . . . relax . . . this has got nothing to do with you!

Don't get me wrong. I still believe in leadership 1.0 – this is not a case of "off with their heads, viva la revolution" . . . it is not a case of "either/or" but of "both/and". And when that happens in an effective way, you get Leadership 4.0 – a dynamic of leadership embracing 1.0, plus 2.0, plus 3.0. And once you have a 4.0 mindset you ask more powerful questions. For example, instead of asking "How can we motivate and engage our people more?" (a typical 1.0 question), one asks "What are we doing that demotivates and disengages, and how can we stop doing that?" (a 4.0 question).

And when you get leadership 4.0, leadership 1.0 looks different – less time managing, more time enabling, less time measuring, more time developing. This is a DYNAMIC view of

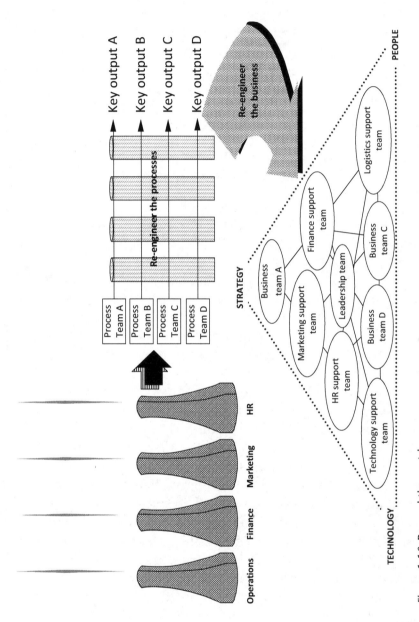

Figure 1.10 Beyond the matrix

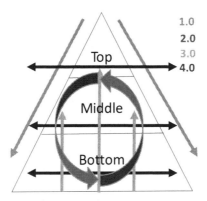

Figure 1.11 Leadership 4.0

leadership, not the traditional static view (which sees leadership only done by leaders in a position or role with defined competencies etc.).

What we need therefore is a dynamic science to help us understand how this dynamic can work because the application of the traditional deterministic science (upon which 90%+ of management/leadership theory is based) is perhaps still necessary but by no means sufficient . . . and certainly does not help you when things get very dynamic.

Without a knowledge of that science, what leaders do to keep on top of all of this VUCA stuff is to be very, very busy . . . doing a whole load of stuff which is just not needed. If one applies only the traditional management science, taught to MBAs, within a 4.0 world you will be unnecessarily busy!

Let's find out what Complexity Science is and how it might give some clues . . . but before we do, some things to think about:

1 How much time are you spending leading downwards (1.0), leading sideways and outwards (2.0) and leading upwards (3.0)?
2 What is the best mix of your time re. 1.0, 2.0 and 3.0? You might want to revisit this question when you finish the book.

3   How can you encourage your reports to exercise more 2.0?
4   How can you encourage your reports to exercise more 3.0?
5   How dynamic is the leadership you exercise (4.0) e.g. to what extent do you follow those you lead, and do they lead you, and to what extent is your boss being led by you as well as you by your boss?

Having considered these questions, you may have identified some actions. We use the KISS model. This is known by some as Keep It Short and Simple, or Keep It Simple, Stupid – but we have another definition, so consider the questions below and jot down some answers:

- What are the things you should KEEP doing?
- What are the things you do not do enough of so should INCREASE?
- What are the things you can START doing?
- And the real payback is from: What are the things you should STOP doing?

References

Bradford, L. and Grossman R.S. (1993), *"Excess Volatility" on the London Stock Market, 1870–1990*, University of California paper, Berkley.

Collins, J. (2001), *Good to Great – Why Some Companies Make the Leap and Others Don't*, New York: Harper Business.

Collins J. and Porras, J. (1997), *Built to Last – Successful Habits of Visionary Companies*, New York: Harper Business.

Hazy, James K., Goldstein, Jeffrey A. and Lichtenstein, Benyamin B. (2007), *Complex Systems Leadership Theory – New Perspectives from Complexity Science on Social and Organizational Effectiveness*, Mansfield: ISCE Publishing.

Heifitz, R. (2013) NPR Interview, online: https://www.npr.org/2013/11/11/230841224/lessons-in-leadership-its-not-about-you-its-about-them

Hirschhorn, L. and Gilmore, T. (1992), "The New Boundaries of the 'Boundaryless' Company", *Harvard Business Review*, May–June.

Magee, R.R. (ed.) (1998) *Strategic Leadership Primer*, Department of Command, Leadership and Management, US Army War College, Carlisle Barracks, PA.

Surowiecki, J. (2004), *The Wisdom of Crowds*, New York: Doubleday.

Wilton, Rose F. (1990), "A new age for business?", *Fortune Magazine*, 8 October.

2 *WHAT new science can help*

Most of the approaches we use in leadership today are based on deterministic thinking – if you do X you should get Y result. Analyse and then, if possible, turn it into a process. Deterministic science has been around a long time, and it still works. However, when things get dynamic and uncertain it does not work so well. So, we need to add another scientific approach to when things are very dynamic and VUCA. Most have not heard of Complexity Science. Some have heard of Chaos Mathematics and most have heard of the butterfly effect. The butterfly effect is a subset of Chaos Mathematics, which is the mathematic sub-set of Complexity Science, which also draws on other "hard" sciences like physics, chemistry and biology. This is a new hard science, and not one dreamed up by some pot-smoking hippies on a far-away beach.

Before we understand how to apply some of the principles, we need to define complexity. The most useable way is that of David Snowden and Mary Boone (2007), called the "Cynefin" model (a Welsh word pronounced "keneven"). It proposes that there are four contexts or issues one deals with: Simple, Complicated, Complex and Chaotic. These can be laid out on a continuum of predictability, where cause and effect can be linked and defined.

Let's look at each, and the traps they hold in VUCA times:

1   **The Simple** – this is where cause and effect are known and outcomes predictable. I would not call manufacturing simple, but in this model the concept is you have raw materials coming into a big box (aka factory) and one can predict

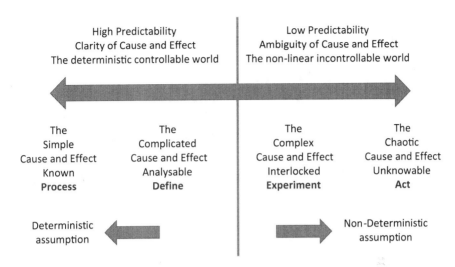

Figure 2.1 Complexity positioned

what comes out. It is not random. Toshiba employees do not wake up and say "Hey, I wonder what will come out of the factory today?". The mistakes we make here in a VUCA environment are two-fold:

a   We tend to try to make everything simple and work hard to turn everything into a process. That ends up with lots of processes trying to maintain the wonderful illusion of control, but when things are dynamic with so many processes, employees are either completely disempowered or (fortune favours the brave) they must work hard to ignore or "work around" the process.

b   We add unnecessary complexity to processes, which then become almost unworkable. So, the lesson here is not to simplify the complex – it is to simplify the simple! Put another way – simplifying the complex is NOT the answer (see point 3 below).

2   **The Complicated** – this where cause and effect, after detailed analysis, can be determined, and a clear decision made with a degree of confidence re the outcome, due to the analysed predictability. The mistakes commonly made here are:

a   Overanalysing and spending too much time on the CONTENT – the WHAT – and too little time on the methodology of implementation – the HOW. This is the famous "content trap" where you get dragged down into the detail, where people are far more comfortable.

b   Analysing fully the complex is largely a waste of time – by the time the analysis is done, the variables may have changed!

And now we have a big jump from the predictable, controllable, deterministic world to the unpredictable, non-linear VUCA world.

3   **The Complex** – this is where all the variables are so interlinked that it is very difficult to predict with any degree of accuracy. There is some predictability – for example the weather is a complex system: we can predict hotter in the summer, colder in the winter and around 30 degrees in Singapore, more or less. But it is hard to predict medium term. So, what is needed is probing experimentation with feedback loops – a dynamic approach. The common traps here are:

a   Trying to control and "get a grip" when this often ends up getting the opposite effect.

b   Using Key Performance Indicators (KPIs) and determined targets which also often get the opposite effect as people invariably play the numbers to do things right, instead of doing the right things.

c   Spending time talking about the WHAT (e.g. trying to clarify cause and effect) rather than the HOW (e.g. how the team will address the issue they are facing).

4   **The Chaotic** – this is where there is no cause and effect. This is perhaps the easiest for leadership – just use one's intuition to do something and act (and, as there is no cause and effect, do not worry too much what that action is!). In reality the chaotic does not exist in organisations for long. The common traps here are:

a   Thinking something is chaotic when in fact it is complex. Complexity viewed from a deterministic mindset can seem to be chaotic.

b   Trying to analyse cause and effect where none exist!

In reality, the simple, the complicated and the complex co-exist in organisations. The trick is to recognise each when faced by them and then take the right approach: for the simple, define and follow a process; for the complicated, analyse and then solve or move to the simple with a process; and for the complex, experiment (more on that later and the use of the butterfly effect).

So, some quick questions to consider:

1   Of 100% of your time leading, what % time do you spend between the simple, the complicated and the complex? If you think you also spend time on the chaotic, add that to the number for the complex because that is probably what it is!

2   How much time do you think you should be spending on each? You may want to revisit your answer here after finishing the book.

3   What do you need to STOP in some areas in order to start in others, if your time spent in each is not optimal?

OK, so far so good – we have begun to define complexity by comparing it to other states. But what about complexity itself, and the science? Where did complexity science come from and what can we learn and apply from it?

Complexity Science emerged in the 1970s when a variety of scientists, all working in splendid isolation within the own fields, began to find the same thing regarding non-linear dynamics (although some would argue the science can be traced further back than that). By the early 1980s there was a lot of commonality emerging, and the first formal institute was formed in 1984 in Santa Fe. Today there are numerous (over 50) institutes around the world studying complex systems. In summary, from a pragmatic leadership perspective, there is some bad news and some good news:

1   First the bad news:

   a   Complex systems are messy – get over it!
   b   They are unpredictable – so learn to go with the flow and be agile
   c   They have "waste" – nature is complex, and birth is a natural thing – if you have witnessed a birth there is a lot of mess and waste (although I've been told some do make placenta pie, believe it or not . . .)

2   There is good news! Complex systems have:

   a   A few simple rules underpinning the complexity
   b   Emergence as a common phenomenon – in other words patterns and solutions can emerge
   c   Things that appear random are not necessarily so
   d   Misalignment, which is not a problem
   e   Inherent self-organisation

There are lots of examples in complexity science that demonstrate the good news, but I have a favourite two. The first is from chaos mathematics and fractals. A couple of examples – the most picturesque is Benoit Mandelbrot's. His simple formula, $Z_{n+1} = Z_n^2 + C$, generates an emergent complex pattern.

If you want to see this amazing complex pattern in action a five-minute video can be seen at: https://www.youtube.com/watch?v=aSg2Db3jF_4

There are a lot of spooky things about Complexity Science – after watching the video you might not be surprised to learn that at around the same time as Mandelbrot discovered this fractal, LSD (completely separately) hit the streets . . .

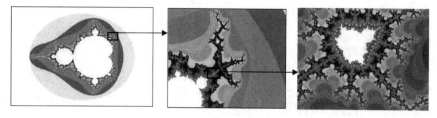

Figure 2.2 The amazing Mandelbrot Set

Figure 2.3 Sierpinski from a triangle

For those who are not into LSD experiences, a simpler fractal is from the Polish mathematician, Sierpinski. Take a triangle, dissect each line and remove the centre, and then repeat several times – a complex pattern emerges.

If we take the same rule, and apply it to a completely different shape we get the same similar result:

What does this mean for a team or organisation? Well you can imagine the "square" team being told they need to achieve the result of the "triangle" team; "We can't do that! We are squares and have years of that tradition!" – well maybe one can. What the science shows is that applying the rules (the HOW) from one context to another completely different, one can get broadly the same result.

Ah ha! I hear you cry – this is still a linear process! But the same can be achieved by a random one – have a look at: https://www.youtube.com/watch?v=kbKtFN71Lfs Things that appear random are not necessarily so. Figure 2.5 below shows what is explained in the video.

The second example from complexity science that I like is from birds flocking. You may have seen this in nature.

Figure 2.4 Sierpinski from a square

After 60 roles of the dice.........   After 600 roles of the dice.........   After 6,000 roles of the dice.........

Figure 2.5 Sierpinski from rolling a dice

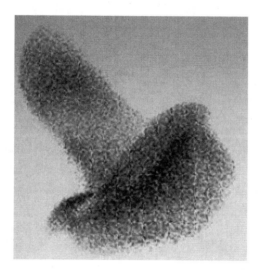

Figure 2.6 Birds flocking

Figure 2.6 shows thousands of birds flocking in a wonderful self-organising way. How do they do that? Where is the leader? In fact, they are following three simple rules discovered by Craig Reynolds in the 1990s (who called the resultant simulation Boids):

1   Cohesion – steer towards average centre of flock mates
2   Alignment – steer in direction of flock mates
3   Separation – do not crowd into flock mates

Notice anything strange about the rules? Two of them are opposites – cohesion and separation. The science gives another clue about complexity – alignment works well when things are complicated, but when things are complex an element of misalignment is needed. This gives space and diversity for the agents in the system to work things out for themselves. A huge amount of time is wasted by leaders in a VUCA environment trying to get alignment on everything.

If you want to see how this works for the birds there is a great short video about Boids at: https://www.youtube.com/watch?v=QbUPfMXXQIY Self-organisation can occur on the basis of a few simple rules, if leaders in the system allow it to emerge.

So what? Well, imagine if the team you led was in fact self-organising – what would that mean for you? More time to lead sideways (leadership 2.0) and upwards (leadership 3.0). More time to develop and coach your people further, enhancing performance and thus playing the leadership 1.0 approach in a very different way. And self-organisation has some key benefits. A recent research project based on some 16,000 employees in 17 countries (published as *The HOW Report* https://howmetrics.lrn.com/) found that on a variety of metrics (e.g. innovation, customer satisfaction, employee engagement, financial performance, reporting misconduct etc.), self-organisation got better results.

So, Complexity Science shows that complex dynamic systems are often based on a few simple rules, that rules from one system can be applied to another for broadly the same result, alignment is not needed, that emergence is key, and that self-organisation is inherent. And self-organisation can get better results.

So much for the science, pretty patterns and birds. What about humans? Can a few simple rules help solve a complex situation without massive leadership effort? And what principles are needed for self-organisation to emerge when allowed by leaders?

Reference

Snowden, D. and Boone, M. (2007), "A Leaders Framework for Decision Making", *Harvard Business Review*, November.

CHAPTER

3 *WHAT principles need to be in place*

We saw in the last chapter that the key payoff for employing complexity science is getting self-organisation. This leads to better results, faster, for less leadership effort by leaders. But how to it? A video "Who needs leaders?" has some clues (https://www.youtube.com/watch?v=ob1yq5hM6qw).

Some 30 people are scattered at random in a large empty space and must pick two people randomly. However, they

Figure 3.1 The Complexity Game

cannot indicate in anyway who those two people are. And then, following a few simple rules, everyone, at the same time, must position themselves at equal distance from the two people they have picked (who have picked another two people, who have picked another two people etc. etc. times 30!). How long do you think that would take? It is certainly complex with more circular references than the great goddess Excel herself would struggle to cope with. Some think it impossible and that there will be a continual loop, like birds flocking. In the video, it takes less than a minute to solve (and having done this with hundreds of groups, less than three minutes). Everyone laughs at the end when asked "What would have happened if we had put one of you in charge?". Why do they laugh? Because it is clear that not only would leadership 1.0 get sub-optimal results, taking a lot more time for a lot more effort, but the more complex things are the less determined, planned and directive leadership 1.0 is needed. The other underlying lesson here is that organisations have largely a 1.0 mindset, within an increasing 4.0 VUCA world, and are very busy trying to keep on top of everything (which is largely a waste of time).

That exercise also demonstrates the few simple principles that need to be in place for self-organisation to occur. They number eight and are organised into two sets – four "hard" and four "soft". The principles are positioned on the Chinese Taoist "Yin-Yang" figure. The reason for that is we need to think "both/and" rather than "either/or". In the West we typically have a very deterministic "either/or" upbringing – Right vs Wrong, God vs the Devil, Heaven vs Hell, etc. etc. The Chinese Taoists see the co-existence of opposites as the very dynamic of life. And the Chinese have a way of thinking that helps this – it is no accident that the first modern mass industrial example of self-organisation was the building of railways across America in the 19th century. In 1864, the Central Pacific Railroad Company ran an experiment where Chinese work teams had their hierarchical (leadership 1.0) control removed and they had to self-organise. They quickly managed to outperform, laying 10 miles of tracks per day (a record that apparently still stands). The other railway

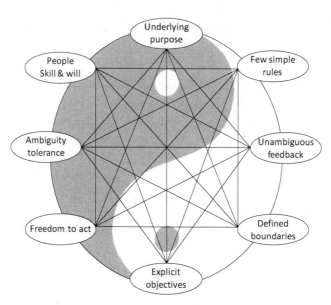

Figure 3.2 Yin/Yang eight principles

companies quickly followed the approach (although they very much reverted to leadership 1.0 when the tracks had been laid!).

So, what are the principles that enabled that exercise to happen in a self-organised way, which we use to demonstrate the simple principles needed for a team and organisation to become self-organising? Note, this is only half the story! Even if these principles are in place, if the boss does not enable leadership 4.0, and sticks only with 1.0, the potential is not released (more about this in the next chapter!).

• Underlying purpose – there is an implicit and unifying underlying purpose to the exercise. When we run this exercise, it is part of a company leadership development programme. We do not need to remind people they are wanting to learn new things – it is the underlying purpose that unites people and thus it is easy for us to ask people to do a strange exercise which some will feel is impossible. If we had all been strangers on a bus, then the underlying purpose would not support the exercise (i.e. wanting to go somewhere and not get off the bus to do a crazy exercise, no matter how insightful the learning). Companies and teams that have a strong but implicit uniting purpose can use it as a guiding light, especially when things become VUCA. It is no accident that this principle is at the top of all the rest. The unifying purpose can be simple: Disney's is "Make people happy", GSK's is "To help people do more, feel better and live longer". Organisations who say their purpose is to maximise shareholder value inevitably underperform – shareholder value is one important result, not a unique purpose!

- Clear individual objective – each person has a very clear idea of what they are trying to achieve. Although they cannot say exactly where they will be, how far from their reference point they will end up or even how (i.e. the route) they will get there, the objective they have is clear enough to get them moving. Note the objective is specific enough to give a clear indication if it is achieved or not, but not so specific as to tie the individual down (for example the angle and distance, as well as the route, are flexible). It would be very counter-productive to even try to specify the detail of the objective! How many times do we fall into the trap of trying to fathom out the objective to the "Nth degree"? Although this can work well for relatively simple tasks and projects, when things are complex and dynamic such detailed working out of the objective does not help at all. In fact, it gets in the way, taking up time and demotivating those involved. So, the objective setting is two-way – the objective setting criteria are set, whilst the individual sets his own. Leadership 1.0 uses "SMART" objectives, but these can be pretty dumb when the situation is complex. What is sufficient is that each individual knows what needs to be achieved and, as important, will know when it has been achieved. As the situation changes, and if that achievement then is lost, the individual has enough clarity to adjust and adapt. Each individual has a sense of ownership of their own objective, as they could choose which two people were their reference points.

- Few simple rules – the rules are sufficient to enable effective action, and enough to keep the system from descending into too much chaos. However, they are not so many as to cause the system to slow down and become cumbersome. The balance between having enough rules to fulfil obligations and allowing enough freedom to act is a fine one. The Disney Corporation found that it had gone too far down the route of having rules and procedures for everything. When they tried to move their concept to Europe and a new Disneyworld in France they found that it did not work. This experience then forced them to look at how they used rules and procedures in general. This saw a major simplification and the results which flowed enabled the new resort to stay afloat, and the current resorts to improve their operations. This move from a heavily measured organisation to a more complex adaptive one is also mirrored in the evolution of Semco in Brazil. This is described in the book called *Maverick*, by their CEO Ricardo Semler (1993).

- Clear boundary – the boundary gives a definition where the action is. For the exercise the boundary is both the area within which it takes place, as well as the boundary of how the game is to be played (i.e. by looking at the two reference points and then moving following the rules to adjust one's position). Organisations typically define boundaries as "who-is-in-charge-of-who", with the "organigram" being the all too typical way of showing how the organisation is structured. Rather than focusing on the boundaries within the organisation, and jealously guarding them as per leadership 1.0, leadership 4.0 looks at the nature of the relationships ACROSS the boundaries outside of the organisation as well as across the internal ones. This is a different way of looking at things – typically organisations focus on the objects within a network (the departments, units, individuals etc.). The other way of looking at it is by seeing the relationships as the main thing, with the objects as the background, as illustrated by Figure 3.3.

  At a more macro level, the boundary conditions of an organisation also include its strategy – what does it deliver, to

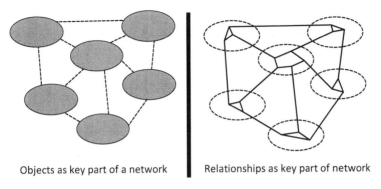

Objects as key part of a network | Relationships as key part of network

Figure 3.3 Not objects – networks!

who and how? Under the leadership 1.0 assumption, strategy is something defined by the leaders and executed by the followers. Under a leadership 4.0 assumption, strategy is defined by the dynamic of the relationships and eco-system within which the organisation exists. At the end of the day, that dynamic needs to be clarified, so the techniques used in clarification may be the same as within a 1.0 assumption, although the process may differ (e.g. the use of mass intervention techniques). The establishment and maintenance of boundary conditions takes time. Whilst in the more traditional days of 1.0 a leader is looking down into the organisation and defining the strategy and resultant organisation, the 4.0 leader will be looking across and outside the organisation, realising that his organisation is itself a node in a complex network.

- Continuous feedback – every individual knows at any time where they are in relationship to achieving their objective. And they are able to interpret the data they see – in other words they can judge distance. They "sense" what the reference points are doing and "respond" – a very real experience of being adaptive. This relates to KPIs. There are huge debates over the use of measurement, both what should be measured, how it should be done and how reported. Suffice it here to say that an organisation needs a range of measures and each individual needs to both understand them and to understand how they influence them. These should not only include "hard" measures such as financial and operational metrics but also "soft" measures ranging from staff attitude (at an organisational level) to personal behavioural 360 feedback (at an individual level). Leadership 1.0 is very much focused on KPIs (i.e. WHAT people do and achieve). Leadership 4.0 focuses more on values (i.e. HOW people operate and behave).

- Discretion and freedom of action – each person is free to act without having to wait for "permission", nor needing guidance on which way to go. This takes both an organisational culture and a personal attitude which takes to heart Stuart's Law of Retroaction (it is easier to seek forgiveness than obtain permission). Having discretion and freedom of action within well-defined boundaries is critical for complexity to work. And people need to feel confident in taking risks and empowered to take initiatives to cross boundaries.

- Ambiguity and uncertainty – within the exercise there is a degree of seeming chaos (which is in fact complex self-organisation) and the situation seems to be one that is far from equilibrium. Whilst for some, if not all, there may be an uncomfortable feeling that things are looking chaotic, and that the exercise may be impossible, people still enter into the flow. This is "far from equilibrium". Uncertainty is the very essence of life itself and is natural and something to be embraced rather than avoided, even if we prefer order and control. And the paradox is that we should not abandon order and control either!

- Skill/will of participants – each person has the ability to judge the distance and move accordingly (skill) and also wants to do the exercise (will). Translated into organisational terms this would mean each person has the skills needed to do their job as well as the motivation to do it well. Again, the field of skills development and motivation theory is a huge area. Suffice it here to say that people are generally more skilled and motivated than their leaders would often suppose (if the stories are anything to go by, as explored in

Chapter 8). The best way a 1.0 leader can develop personal skills to move to 4.0, as well as the skills of followers, is to ensure a process of knowledge transfer is available, as well as spending time coaching and employing necessary development courses. And the best way a 4.0 leader can develop motivation is to understand how leadership behaviour can demotivate – and then eradicate such behaviour! This issue is explored further in the application of the skill/will model in the next chapter. It explores not only the skill/will of followers, but also that of leaders as well.

Although there are eight principles they can combine in thousands of possible ways. For example, Dan Pink's research shows motivation is created by linking just some of the principles: Purpose, Skill (Mastery) and Freedom (Autonomy). A fun video, explaining this and which outlines his book *Drive: The Surprising Truth About What Motivates Us* (2009), can be seen at: https://www.youtube.com/watch?v=u6XAPnuFjJc

So how is your team and organisation doing? Here is a questionnaire for you to do – fill it in and then add up the scores (circle only ONE number for each question).

Table 3.1 Test how your team and organisation are doing

1   People in the organisation/team have a strong shared sense of common purpose.

Strongly disagree	Disagree	Neutral	Agree	Strongly agree
1 or 2	3 or 4	5 or 6	7 or 8	9 or 10

2   Each individual has clear, measurable individual objectives.

Strongly disagree	Disagree	Neutral	Agree	Strongly agree
1 or 2	3 or 4	5 or 6	7 or 8	9 or 10

(continued)

Table 3.1 (continued)

3 People are encouraged to take the initiative and act on opportunities when they arise.

Strongly disagree	Disagree	Neutral	Agree	Strongly agree
1 or 2	3 or 4	5 or 6	7 or 8	9 or 10

4 The boundaries of responsibilities between people and teams/departments are clear.

Strongly disagree	Disagree	Neutral	Agree	Strongly agree
1 or 2	3 or 4	5 or 6	7 or 8	9 or 10

5 People are well qualified and skilled to do their work.

Strongly disagree	Disagree	Neutral	Agree	Strongly agree
1 or 2	3 or 4	5 or 6	7 or 8	9 or 10

6 The rules of the organisation/team are clear and understood by all.

Strongly disagree	Disagree	Neutral	Agree	Strongly agree
1 or 2	3 or 4	5 or 6	7 or 8	9 or 10

7 There is an effective, well-defined process for continuous feedback.

Strongly disagree	Disagree	Neutral	Agree	Strongly agree
1 or 2	3 or 4	5 or 6	7 or 8	9 or 10

8 Although there is an element of ambiguity, things still seem to work well.

Strongly disagree	Disagree	Neutral	Agree	Strongly agree
1 or 2	3 or 4	5 or 6	7 or 8	9 or 10

9 The organisation/team has a shared idea of its contribution to society/the wider organisation.

Strongly disagree	Disagree	Neutral	Agree	Strongly agree
1 or 2	3 or 4	5 or 6	7 or 8	9 or 10

10 Everybody knows what is expected of them and what they have to achieve.

Strongly disagree	Disagree	Neutral	Agree	Strongly agree
1 or 2	3 or 4	5 or 6	7 or 8	9 or 10

11 People are free to decide how to do their work and do not feel controlled.

Strongly disagree	Disagree	Neutral	Agree	Strongly agree
1 or 2	3 or 4	5 or 6	7 or 8	9 or 10

12 It is clear to team members who they need to cooperate with across boundaries.

Strongly disagree	Disagree	Neutral	Agree	Strongly agree
1 or 2	3 or 4	5 or 6	7 or 8	9 or 10

13 People have a high degree of motivation.

Strongly disagree	Disagree	Neutral	Agree	Strongly agree
1 or 2	3 or 4	5 or 6	7 or 8	9 or 10

14 The rules of the organisation/team are few but effective.

Strongly disagree	Disagree	Neutral	Agree	Strongly agree
1 or 2	3 or 4	5 or 6	7 or 8	9 or 10

15 There is a degree of uncertainty about how things are achieved, but objectives are met.

Strongly disagree	Disagree	Neutral	Agree	Strongly agree
1 or 2	3 or 4	5 or 6	7 or 8	9 or 10

16 Individuals know how well they are doing towards achieving their objectives at any given time.

Strongly disagree	Disagree	Neutral	Agree	Strongly agree
1 or 2	3 or 4	5 or 6	7 or 8	9 or 10

So how did you score? The following is a broad guide for the total score:

- More than 120 = Excellent
- 100 – 120 = Good – some areas may need attention
- 60 – 100 = Danger zone – identify weak areas and address
- 30 – 60 = Severe danger – take action to safeguard
- Less than 30 = Still there?

A more detailed report, showing the scores for each principle as well as the balance between Yin and Yang (if you are at more than 2% difference between each it is out of balance) is available at: https://www.complexadaptiveleadership.com/self-assessment/

Since the original best-selling book detailing all of this came out in 2010, *Complex Adaptive Leadership: Embracing Paradox and Uncertainty* (CAL), some independent research has looked at the CAL approach and linked it to performance. In the USA, independent research by Oliver Wyman (2013) looked at an industry and picked some of the major competitors retrospectively to see if financial performance is correlated with

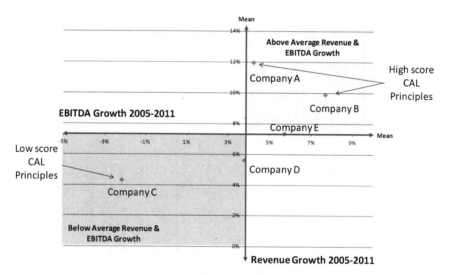

Figure 3.4 CAL principles and EBITDA/revenue growth

a strong presence of the CAL principles. Figure 3.4 shows the summary results.

A few years later in Russia some analysis was done at the team level. This looked at project teams, as well as individuals working outside teams, and looked at performance on a few levels. Needless to say, individuals working outside of teams did not perform as well as those in teams, but the teams that had a high component of the CAL principles did best of all.

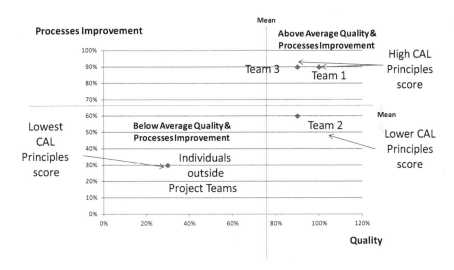

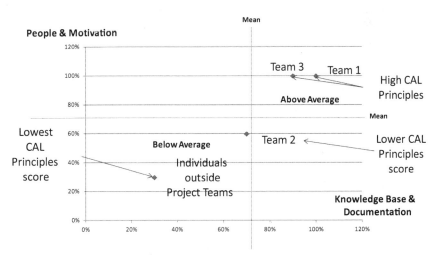

Figure 3.5 CAL principles and team performance

Here are some questions to reflect on regarding each of the eight principles:

1   Purpose:

    a   How can you connect your team to the wider organisational purpose?

    b   What is the unique purpose that your team plays for the organisational benefit and how can you make that a sense of pride and ownership?

2   Objectives:

    a   How can you enable your team to set their own "stretch" objectives to allow more accountability?

    b   How can you ensure your team have a say in setting objectives so to improve accountability and ownership?

3   Skill/will:

    a   How are you developing your team to enable their skills and performance to increase?

    b   What exists that demotivates your team and what can you do to remove it?

4   Few simple rules:

    a   What are the few, simple, rules that your team need to follow to enable self-organisation to occur?

    b   What rules and procedures forced onto your team get in the way and how can you change that?

5   Ambiguity:

    a   When dealing with a complex issue, to what extent can your team live with a good-enough solution rather than try to over-engineer everything to eradicate uncertainty?

    b   How can you encourage confidence in your team when surrounded by a VUCA environment?

6   Feedback:

    a   How can you ensure that each team member has the measurement and transparency needed to gauge progress and performance?

b   How can you improve the transparency of the numbers that matter and the ability to understand them?

7   Boundaries:

a   If you imagine your team as a node in a network (instead of a hierarchical fiefdom), what are the connections across boundaries that are critical and how can you solidify the connections?

b   How much time do you spend practicing 2.0 (across functional boundaries) and 3.0 (upwards across hierarchical boundaries) and how much time should you be doing this?

8   Freedom:

a   How much freedom do you enable your team with in deciding how they solve issues, and what can you do to hold back and encourage more?

b   What gets in the way of self-organisation and what can you do to remove those barriers?

Most teams and organisations get a good score – which means there is much potential that can be released. Sadly, such potential is neither recognised nor released as leaders are stuck in the 1.0 mindset. What is needed then is a simple yet effective way at looking at the choices of leadership behaviour. We have already seen that if you practice 1.0 in a 4.0 reality then you will end up like a hamster on a wheel – being busy but going nowhere fast. Time to start thinking about jumping off the wheel and "getting on the balcony" – let's look at the HOW side of the equation.

But before we do – the last two chapters may have opened some new ideas:

- What are the things you should KEEP doing?
- What are the things you do not do enough of and so should INCREASE?
- What are the things you can START doing?
- What are the things you should STOP doing?

References

Obolensky, N. (2010), *Complex Adaptive Leadership – Embracing Paradox and Uncertainty*, Farnham: Gower Applied Research.

Pink, D.H. (2009), *Drive – The Surprising Truth About What Motivates Us*, Hull: Riverhead Books.

Semler, R. (1993), *Maverick – The Success Story Behind the World's Most Unusual Workplace*, New York: Warner.

Wyman, O. (2013), "Cracking the Organizational Code for Growth", paper presented at the 4th Annual Aviation and Aerospace Industry Manufacturing Summit, October 16–18, Texas.

CHAPTER 4

HOW to get it done – an overview

The last chapter showed the principles needed for self-organisation to work. But that is only half the story. Based on over 3,000 measurements in 40 organisations around the world we have found that many have these principles, more or less, in place. What is missing is the needed behaviours by leaders to enable better performance. Analysis has found two major problems typically occur. But before we look at those problems, we need to cover a couple of things, and do some exploration!

First, we need to position how you apply 1.0 leadership. Remember it is still needed, as part of the 4.0 dynamic. We position this not as a style or competence but as a MINDFUL CHOICE OF BEHAVIOUR, within a new mindset. Hopefully the preceding chapters have begun to widen your mindset about what leadership is. This chapter looks at the behaviours, or strategies, you can mindfully employ.

Second, we need to have a map to help us be more mindful. To do this we will use one of the eight Yin-Yang principles (or 4+4 as we call them) – skill/will. This can be used from two viewpoints:

1   The skill and will of the people you lead to get the job done and meet what is needed to achieve in a fully accountable way and
2   YOUR skill and will both to develop your people and also to achieve the goals being pursued by your team.

To start the exploration please fill in this questionnaire and score card below, which looks at the choices of behaviour you might make given a range of scenarios.

This should not take long. Assume you are the leader of a team. It does not necessarily have to be the team you are currently in, if you have one. Imagine you are in the circumstances described. Read the possible responses. Do not think too long about which one you would choose. Circle/tick one of the responses that you think you most likely would do (as opposed to could or should!). Use the scoring table at the end to identify your score.

1 Your team is faced with a change of circumstance for which team members are poorly experienced and unprepared. They don't want to adapt to the new context.

   a   Tell them that they must adapt and show them clearly what needs to be done.

   b   Inform them about the benefits that the change will bring (including the new skills they will gain from the training arranged), and point out the cost of not adapting.

   c   Ask them how they propose to deal with the new situation and give what they say serious thought.

   d   Keep an eye on the situation, but do not interfere.

2 A subordinate of yours is keen to move ahead. However, he does not know how to implement the new procedures put in place. He is concerned as performance might suffer.

   a   Point out how the new procedures will improve both the situation and the team's environment, and how he will benefit.

   b   Seek his views as to how the new procedures should be implemented and consider his recommendations.

   c   Do not get involved yet and wait and see what happens.

   d   Show him clearly how the new procedures can be followed and ensure more detailed training is done if he needs it.

3   A difficult state of affairs has occurred, but, despite him having the ability, you have detected a distinct lack of willingness by one of your subordinates to deal with it.

   a   Ask him what the problems/barriers are and seek his recommendations for solutions.
   b   Let him work it out for himself and do not interfere unless performance suffers.
   c   Inform him that you have detected his lack of willingness, that this is unacceptable and he must deal with the situation.
   d   Point out penalties for failure and offer him a small bonus to ensure success.

4   New changes are underway. Your motivated team is coping well, but you are concerned that performance may suffer without further guidance.

   a   Do nothing yet – monitor the situation and be prepared to step in if performance or motivation begins to decline.
   b   Remind them of what the new changes are and the expectations of how the team should act.
   c   Reiterate how the new changes will benefit all concerned and what the penalties of failure could be.
   d   Arrange a team meeting to voice your concerns and ask them how they can sustain their current performance.

5   Morale is high despite a rapid change of direction. However, your team does not yet have the new skills they will need and performance is starting to suffer.

   a   Show them how things have got better since the change of direction.
   b   Ask them how they propose to deal with the change of direction.
   c   Do not get involved but wait for the training programme for the team to deliver.
   d   Take action to let them know precisely how they need to change working practices and quickly bring forward the training course.

6 A new change is needed and one of your subordinates is unhappy about it – he does not want to change nor upgrade his skills to do the new work. You have already arranged a training course to deliver the new skills that the team will need.

   a Ask him to identify what the barriers are and how he proposes to overcome them.

   b Be careful not to do anything unless the situation gets worse.

   c Reiterate what the new changes are, that there are no other options and that training is arranged for him.

   d Stress the benefits of the new training course and how the changes will improve the situation and help avoid a worsening situation.

7 A change in procedures needs your team to adapt. They have the skills to deal with the new system but one of your subordinates is resisting the need to change.

   a Avoid confrontation and see if she changes her attitude.

   b Take firm and swift action to tell her what is needed in clear terms.

   c Demonstrate how the new procedures have simplified her work and indicate the down side of non-compliance.

   d Ask what the barriers to change are and how she can overcome them.

8 Challenging targets are being met with hard work and morale is high. Your team seems happy but you are worried that one of your subordinates might need more help.

   a Tell her how she can best meet the targets and how to improve.

   b Remind her of the benefits that will accrue when the targets are met and suggest further improvements.

   c Ask her how performance can be improved further and what needs to be put in place.

   d Leave her to continue her good work and relax a bit more.

9 Your highly skilled team has been efficient and performed well, but you have seen signs that motivation is beginning to drop, and this will soon affect performance.

   a   Arrange a fun offsite which includes a workshop to identify problems and opportunities to improve the situation.

   b   Tell them they need to improve motivation and in clear terms what the expectations are.

   c   Do nothing yet – monitor the situation and be prepared to step in if performance is affected.

   d   Point out the benefits currently achieved as well as the penalties which may ensue if performance suffers.

10 Your team is doing well and seems happy to meet the stretch targets that you have set. However, you are worried that one of your subordinate's performance might suffer without further motivation because of a recent family bereavement.

   a   Keep an eye on him but do not interfere yet and be less worried.

   b   Remind him of the consequence of failure and negative outcomes which may arise, as well as the benefits which will accrue if he succeeds.

   c   Tell him of your concerns and inform him again of what needs to be done.

   d   Ask him how motivation can further be improved and consider his recommendations.

11 Your team is highly motivated, but a rapid introduction of new systems has seen productivity suffer and this will soon affect morale.

   a   Get an expert to show them how to use the system in a customised training session, and identify further training needs.

   b   Seek their recommendations for how better to use the system.

c   Reiterate how damaging it is not to use the system in the correct way, point out the benefits and arrange a training session.

d   Let them work it out and do not get involved.

12 There is a pressing need for the team to change to a new system and the Change Management team has arranged a training course for them. However, one of your subordinates does not want to change nor attend the course.

a   Inform her of the benefits of change and the training she will soon receive, as well as the cost of not changing.

b   Wait until her performance is affected further before taking action.

c   Arrange a longer meeting with her to work out solutions to her problems.

d   Tell her she has to change and that she will do the training course.

13 Performance is good, and your team has continued to show their usual high motivation. You feel that you are not contributing enough as their leader.

a   Introduce a new bonus scheme to improve morale and demonstrate your involvement.

b   Do nothing and be careful not to interfere.

c   Tell them that you wish to play a more active role and increase the frequency of their reporting to you.

d   Arrange a team offsite to have some fun but also to identify improvements and how to achieve them.

14 An older subordinate of yours wants to embrace the changes which are planned, but she feels daunted by the demands for the new skills which will be needed.

a   Reiterate how the new changes will improve things, and how the changes will help avoid the downward trend leading to job cuts.

   b   Don't intervene yet and wait to see how she will really cope.

   c   Tell her about the new skills needed and say she will be trained quickly if she needs it.

   d   Ask her how she proposes to overcome the barriers to the new changes.

15 The external situation has changed rapidly, and your team has been left behind, unable to cope. They feel they should quit.

   a   Wait until someone actually quits before taking action.

   b   Inform them of the dire consequences of quitting and that training support is available for those that need it.

   c   Make everyone feel involved and seek their recommendations.

   d   Act quickly and firmly by saying quitting is not an option, and show them in detail what needs to be done.

16 Your subordinates are highly qualified and are well capable of doing a good job. But they have not performed as well as they could and do not seem keen to do so.

   a   Tell them clearly what the targets are and how they can best achieve them.

   b   Ask them why performance is not as good as it can be, and seek their recommendations for how to improve the situation.

   c   Do nothing yet – monitor the situation and be prepared to step in if performance is further adversely affected.

   d   Remind them of the benefits if targets are met.

Scoring sheet

Go back over your answers and circle the relevant response letter you chose in the table below. Then add up the number of responses in each column. The total responses should number 16 (assuming you answered all questions).

Table 4.1 Scoring sheet

Strategy: Question:	1	2	3	4
1	a	b	c	d
2	d	a	b	c
3	c	d	a	b
4	b	c	d	a
5	d	a	b	c
6	c	d	a	b
7	b	c	d	a
8	a	b	c	d
9	b	d	a	c
10	c	b	d	a
11	a	c	b	d
12	d	a	c	b
13	c	a	d	b
14	c	a	d	b
15	d	b	c	a
16	a	d	b	c
Totals:	Strategy 1	Strategy 2	Strategy 3	Strategy 4

So, what's this all about? The questionnaire shows the number of times you chose a particular strategy:

- Strategy 1 – this is the "tell" approach, a "push". Push can be both telling, showing or even sending someone to be trained in a new skill.
- Strategy 2 – this is the "sell" approach, another "push" strategy where ownership is needed. Put another way, if you need people to "buy" in, you need to "sell".

- Strategy 3 – this is the "involve" approach, a "pull" strategy, where the follower has the capability but you need to pull it out.
- Strategy 4 – is the "devolve" approach, another "pull" strategy albeit indirect. This is where you chose to hang back and allow a solution to emerge (presuming there was a problem in the first place!).

Before we get into the scores, let's get an overview of these strategies and how they fit together. We need a roadmap – and we call it the 2+2.

These four strategies (Figure 4.1) can be mapped on a skill/will matrix, looking at the skill and will of the person you are dealing with. Skill can be knowledge and/or competence. Will can be motivation (i.e. want to do something you need them to do) and/or confidence to do it.

Let's see how these strategies can blend and play out. Let's start with the hardest situation – the top right quadrant (low will/low skill). You need someone to do something, but they do not want to do it and nor do they yet have the skill. Rather than trying to fix everything at once, its best to disaggregate and work on one aspect first and then the other. The two options of where to start are:

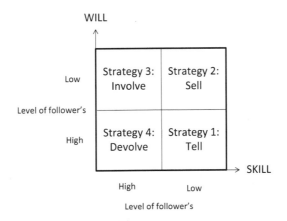

Figure 4.1 Skill/will and the 2+2 strategies

1   Work on the skill part first. This is certainly the Situational Leadership approach, using the "tell" (which could be show how to do, train etc.). That may have worked back in the 1960s, when the Situational Leadership model emerged, but probably would not work so well today. Sending someone to be trained in something they do not want to do in the first place does not make much sense.
2   Work on the will part first. Getting the person to want to do something and when they do, then probably sending them onto a training course when they are motivated would probably get a better result.

Working on the will first is the best bet. But how to "sell"? There are a lot of skills in selling, but in outline most would do the following:

1   Find out from the individual not only why they do not want to do something but also what their hopes, aspirations and wants are (this is called "market research").
2   Align the task that needs to be done to what the individual wants (this is called "product position").
3   Show what is in it for the individual – not features but benefits (as well as the consequence of not doing what needs to be done, called "benefits not features").

At this stage they might say "OK, but I don't know how!". In other words, they have moved to the bottom right quadrant (high will/low skill). Let's imagine in our scenario that this is not a simple task of simply showing them what needs to be done, but some training is needed. So off they go on a training course. On the course they have people with them who have more experience and who frequently challenge the trainer by saying "Yeah, but in real life . . .". This shakes the confidence a little of our follower, who then comes back to "real life"! At this stage their motivation is still high, but their confidence is a bit low. They have moved into the top left quadrant – so the strategy here is a "pull" one – involve. This can take a variety of possible forms from coaching, to mentoring, to supporting the individual until their confidence grows. And once it does, and they have the skill and will do what is needed, you can let go and devolve (which we look at a bit more later).

So far, we have looked at the skill and will of the follower. But what about your skill and will, as well as the need for you to develop people and get goals achieved? Again, the four strategies apply in a slightly different matrix.

This is like the Situational Leadership (SL) model approach (although there are some big differences and CAL 2+2 builds on SL via the skill/will above).

When things are pressing, and you need buy in – sell. But when buy in is not needed then tell can do. When the situation is not so pressing, and you can use it to develop people, then involve. And when there is no value you can add, then step back and get out of the way!

The questionnaire you did will show the number of times you chose each strategy. A perfect score (as far as adaptiveness is concerned) is 4 in each column. Of course you might have been devolving when you should have been selling, and a more comprehensive report (which shows not only how adaptive you are, but also how effective, responsive and balanced your choices are) is available at: https://www.complexadaptiveleadership. com/self-assessment/

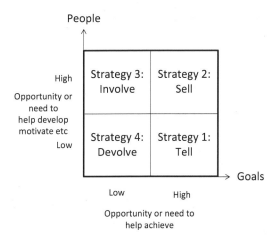

Figure 4.2 People/goals and the 2+2 strategies

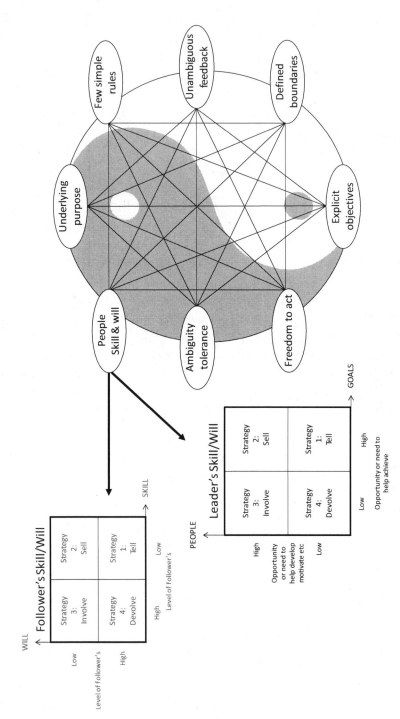

Figure 4.3 Yin-Yang eight linked to the 2+2s

So, in summary we have taken a deep dive into the skill/will part of the eight principles (deep dives in the other seven areas exist, but this is the most important for looking at the HOW).

Having done this questionnaire with thousands of managers around the world a trend has emerged. Broadly speaking the sell and tell side seem to be well catered for – in other words the "push" side of leadership seems to be balanced around the world, although some can do telling and selling better than others. The problem is on the other side of the equation – the "pull" side as the data in Figure 4.4 show (from 2,500 managers from 43 different countries and 22 industries).

There are two problems here:

1   Leaders chose the involve strategy too much. Involvement is nice but:

    a   It takes a lot of time! And why do leaders do too much? Well, going back, one reason could be leaders know they do not know so they get involved to try to keep on top of everything.

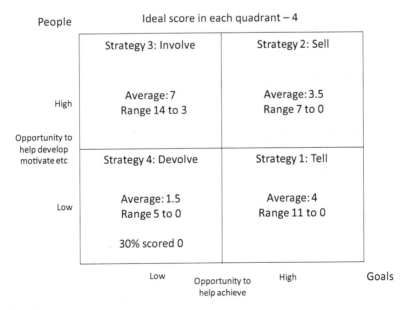

Figure 4.4 CAL 2+2 research findings

b   A bigger issue is that too much involvement looks, from the follower point of view, as micro-managing – and a lot of that is about! Every micro-manager we've met has never seen themselves as such but they all admit getting involved far too much. So, what's the answer? This is linked to the second problem.

2   Leaders do not let go enough. In the data above 30% do not let go at all and 70% do let go enough. Why? Because as things become more complex the leadership 1.0 spasm response is to "get a grip". We saw in Chapter 3 this is NOT what is needed. But if the only science you know is deterministic, and the only leadership you know is based on the 1.0 assumption, that's what's going to happen.

There is also a question of balance – the balance between push (S1 and S2) and pull (S3 and S4), and the balance between physical effort (S2 and S3) and emotional effort (S1 and S4).

The data in Figure 4.4 shows that overall the balance between push and pull is about right. However, the balance between physical effort (it takes more time to sell and involve) and emotional effort (it's harder to tell – for some – or let go – for most) is way out.

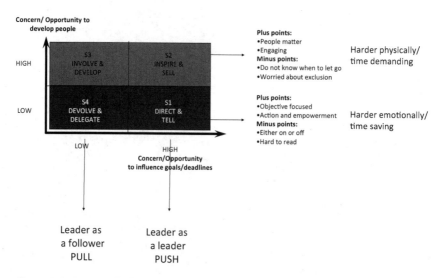

Figure 4.5 CAL 2+2 balance equations

What's the solution? There are two sides to the solution coin. The first side is the leader's side, the second the follower's. Let's look at each in the following two chapters.

Before we do – some questions to reflect on:

1   If your choices are typical (e.g. too much involve not enough devolve), how can you involve less (and that does not mean abandon) and devolve more?
2   How can you get more balance (if needed) between push and pull?
3   How can you get more balance (if needed) between physical and emotional effort?

Also:

- What are the things you should KEEP doing?
- What are the things you do not do enough of and so should INCREASE?
- What are the things you can START doing?
- What are the things you should STOP doing?

5 *HOW to get it done – the leadership issues*

We LOVE excuses to underperform. For example: how many people think they have not enough time? Have you ever said that? This of course is nonsense – you have 60 seconds in the minute, 60 minutes in the hour, 24 hours in the day, 7 days a week, 52 weeks a year. If there is a question of how much time you have, its only how many years do you have left? And that's probably for someone else "up there" to answer! In reality, let's get our feet on the ground and no bullshit: you have all the time in the world. It's not about time; IT'S ABOUT CHOICE. Let me say it again: IT'S ABOUT CHOICE.

The next excuse is "I have no choice. I have to X, Y, Z . . .". Again, one can argue this – you ALWAYS have a choice. Its not about not having choice – its about understanding and either accepting or managing CONSEQUENCE. There are also some other things at play, like ego and delusion. We explore the latter in this chapter.

In the previous chapter we saw that most leaders need to learn when and how to let go. This is not easy. We find that neither reading a detailed (and perhaps too academic) book nor attending a workshop is enough, which is why we designed a fully integrated 70-20-10 programme. This consists of three parts:

- 10% is a kick-off workshop where the basic parts of this book are explored in full with experiential learning, questionnaires and thought experiments. The interaction and discussion amongst participants embeds the learning. Now you don't have that, but there is nothing to stop you getting a few others to read and discuss this book with! And reading this book is your 10%.

- 20% is peer co-coaching. This involves using the CAL coaching approach, described in Chapter 6, in small groups of three to four, which self-organise in our workshops. Again, you don't have that but maybe you can form such a group with the folks in the bullet point above? Meet at least once a month over four months to co-coach each other and share progress.
- 70% is application to the day job and learning how to apply the approach, with making mindful practice and the use of an online tool to log every day for five minutes looking back, and ten minutes each week looking at the busy agenda to plan how to play the week differently. Again, you do not have that, but there is nothing stopping you getting a diary or notebook and doing the same. This is discussed more in the last chapter.

At the end of the book we attempt to replicate this journey for you. As for the more traditional programme, after four months of applied learning and reflective practice, leaders widely report getting better results, faster for less effort by learning when and how to devolve more. A case study (including detailed results and testimonies) of such a programme, which won an international Gold Award for Executive Development, is at: https://www.efmd.org/images/stories/efmd/EIP/2017/GOLD/Nokia_CAL_Abilitie-EFMD_EiP_2017-Submission.pdf

Figure 5.1 CAL Executive Development Gold Award

This book is very much designed to enable you to benefit from the approach without necessarily having to attend a programme customised for your company.

The idea of letting go and allowing self-organisation (natural flow in a complex dynamic) is not new. Here is a quotation from the Taoist philosopher Lao Tzu (translation 1994):

> A leader is best when people barely know that he exists, not so good when people obey and acclaim him, worst when they despise him. Fail to honour people, they fail to honour you. But of a good leader, who talks little, when his work is done, his aims fulfilled, they will all say, "We did this ourselves."

Part of devolving is letting go, not just trying to manage everything, not just trying to keep on top of all the information, but also letting go of the need to boost our own ego. Key to this is the concept of *wu wei* (not doing when doing is unnecessary). So, the concept of enabling self-organisation, enabling self-management, as a leader, is not new! But what is new is, for the first time, we have a science that explains why and when this is necessary, and CAL can help to explain how to exercise it.

But why do leaders not let go? Part of the reason is that there is no understanding of Complexity Science showing when and why it is necessary to let go more; another reason is the fear of uncertainty which leads us to try and keep on top of everything (hopefully the previous chapters have sorted those). But there are a few other reasons. Another quick questionnaire – score each statement below as follows:

If you fully agree with the statement – score 4

If you often agree with the statement – score 3

If you sometimes agree with the statement – score 2

If you rarely agree with the statement – score 1

If you never agree with the statement – score 0

Keep a running score as you go – so 16 questions will have a maximum score of 64.

1 I work best when under pressure
2 I tend to blame external pressures for not spending thinking/reflecting time
3 I am frustrated by slowness around me – hate queues and jams
4 I feel guilty taking time off work
5 I seem to be rushing between places and events
6 I seem to be pushing people away to finish tasks on my plate
7 I feel anxious when out of touch
8 I am often thinking of one thing when doing another
9 I am at my best when handling a crisis
10 The adrenaline from a new crisis is more satisfying than long-term results
11 I give up quality time with important people (e.g. family) to handle a crisis
12 I assume people understand the disappointment of Q11 if I must handle a crisis
13 Solving a crisis gives my day meaning
14 I eat whilst working (lunch etc.)
15 I think that one day I'll be able to do what *I want* to do
16 A list of lots of things ticked off/lots of emails answered etc. makes me feel productive.

So, what's this about? It's about a lot of things, such as work/life balance. But when you come to think about it, what a dreadful term – "work vs life". Life vs death I get. But work vs life? Assumes one is dead at work and fully alive outside (mind you, seeing the faces of some people on their daily commute to work, one wonders!). A better term is work vs family balance. Or work vs own hobbies balance. The questionnaire is also about addiction. Before we define what sort of addiction, let's look at addiction quickly.

Why do people become addicted to things? Simple: it feels good (and you knew that it would)! A reliable, predictable good feeling. And what's the downside? Various things can suffer: health, friendships, family life etc.

So what addiction are we talking about here? I call it the "hamster wheel" addiction, our addiction to action, our addiction to work and urgency. Urgency feels good – we are a hero, we solve things, we handle crisis, we feel valued and important. But addiction to this has downsides – like hamsters on a wheel we are very busy, feeling good about it (every wonder why hamsters like it?), but we end up going nowhere fast. And if we become too addicted bad things happen – we end up with divorce, estranged children, a triple bypass, performance suffers, we get burned out, we end up being sacked and then, bitter and twisted, we die lonely with no-one at the funeral . . . a bit grim and overstated, but you get the general idea. So how addicted, if at all, are you?

The following is a guide:

0–20	Low urgency mindset (anyone there? Or already had the triple bypass?)
20–30	Medium urgency mindset – some urgency mindset is healthy
30–40	Strong urgency mindset – a warning sign, not an addict yet but . . .
40 plus	Urgency addiction
50 plus	Not dead yet?

What does such urgency lead us to do? Basically, it puts what's important at risk and wastes lives (yes, you are alive at work, even if sometimes it doesn't feel like it!). If you have a strong addictive score you are not alone. Most leaders in today's busy world do – but they underperform.

There is some research, using the Eisenhower matrix (subsequently used by Covey, 1994), which looked at where average managers vs high-performing ones spent their time. People spend time at work on things which are urgent and not urgent, as well as things that are important vs not important.

	Urgent	Non urgent
Important	1. Crisis Pressing problem Irate client First aid Help distress Agreed deadline Reacting flexibly	2. Quality Preparation Planning Relationships Re-creation Training Self-development
Not important	3. Deception Interruptions Some meetings Some mail Some phone calls Someone else's importance	4. Waste Gossiping Mindless activities Escape from Q1 Junk mail Time wasters Some phone calls

Figure 5.2 Eisenhower matrix

I always thought that if you spent more time planning (in the quality box) then you get a lot less drama (in the crisis box). However, the research does not bear this out – so no matter how good you are, "Shit happens", as they say. What the research does show is a massive trade-off.

	Urgent	Non urgent
Important	1. Crisis 20% hi-perf (25% avg)	2. Quality 65% hi-perf (15% avg)
Not important	3. Delusion/Illusion 15% hi-perf (55% avg)	4. Waste < 1% hi-perf (5% avg)

Figure 5.3 A world of delusions

The trade-off is between the quality and delusion box. The average leader spends 55% of time in delusion – either self-delusion, in being very busy trying to keep on top of things, or deluded by others. When added to the waste box that means, more or less, 60% of management salary in a company is poured down the drain!

I am sure this pertains to you! For example, how many meetings do you go to wondering "What am I doing here?". Meanwhile, although the top-performing managers still spend some time there, they spend most time in the quality box – focused on the important, not the urgent.

Now some of you might have the excuse: "Yes, this is great but I am micro-managed by my boss who expects me to be on top of everything".

Sorry for the tough love: stop being a victim, start being a leader. Stop being a ball, stand up and become a player. This a classic leadership 3.0 issue for you to resolve with a fanatical 1.0 boss. How to deal with it? Lots of ways, but here are some tips which have worked for others:

1 Think two levels up – if you understand what your boss is getting caught up with, you can put yourself in their shoes!
2 Remember – one person's micro-management is another person's need to be involved – so what is the real need and how can it be managed by you?
3 Demonstrate you understand their position and be proactive.
4 Agree a modus operandi (MO), a routine so their needs are met.
5 Buy the boss a copy of this book!

The leadership angle therefore has looked not only at the choices of behaviour you make, but also how you chose (and yes, am sorry, you ALWAYS have a choice) to spend your time and manage circumstance (such as your boss). Before we look at the followership angle, here are some questions to reflect on:

1 Look at the time you spend – how much time is spent in each box (be honest with yourself).
2 Looking at the delusion box – what can you let go of and devolve? Devolving does not mean passing the can – for example a meeting you regularly attend might be a waste of time for you, but could be a great development opportunity for a subordinate.
3 How will you change the time spent from delusion to quality? You might want to revisit this question after the end of the book.
4 And if you have a micro-managing boss – what will you do about it?

Also:

- What are the things you should KEEP doing?
- What are the things you do not do enough of and so should INCREASE?
- What are the things you can START doing?
- What are the things you should STOP doing?

References

Covey, R.S. (1994), *The 7 Habits Of Highly Effective People. Powerful Lessons on Personal Change*, London: Simon & Schuster.
Tzu, L. (1994), *Tao Te Ching*, trans. M. Kwok, eds M. Palmer and J. Ramsay, Shaftesbury: Element Classical Editions.

CHAPTER *HOW to get it done – the followership issues*

So far so good. But still some issues to address. For example, you might say (unlikely and an extreme example):

> I have a great boss, am aware I spend time in the delusion box and really want to let go and devolve more, even have a perfectly balanced score in the 2+2, but my team just does not want to step up . . . I am surrounded by morons! How can I soar like an eagle when I am tied down by turkeys?

The short answer: you get the followers you deserve and if there is a moron – look in the mirror! You need to nudge them along to step up. The first step is to recognise three things are interlinked:

1   Responsibility – made up of two words: "response" and "ability". What is the skill and will of your followers to be able to respond? This links to the 2+2.
2   Accountability – made up of two words; "account" and "ability". What is the ability of followers to take account of what they are doing? This links to the eight principles.
3   Authority – you cannot make someone responsible and accountable without giving authority.

Organisations are great at putting accountability in one place, responsibility in another and keeping authority in a third place. So, the first step is to look at the balance of those things – these are the contextual aspects of followership.

The next step is to understand where your followers are. Here is a simple way of looking at it. There are various levels of followers (note that this can be as much driven by context – as above, as well as your behaviour as a leader – behaviour breeds behaviour) as well as the individual capability or personality of the individual. Put another way, take a person from one context or organisation, put them in another context or organisation, and their followership behaviour may well change over time.

Level 1 – A follower who just WAITS to be told what to do next. After they finish something they just wait to be directed and are not at all proactive.

Level 2 – a little more proactive – a follower who finishes something and then ASKS to be told.

These two levels should be unacceptable! There is no thinking or engaging brains at all. If you have followers like this, it is your behaviour that has bred them. The fast and fatal response is to tell them what to do. This removes accountability – it is the best-loved tactic of the "Teflon follower" – where nothing sticks! If it all goes pear- shaped, the response is "Sorry boss – just doing what you told me!".

Level 3 – the follower comes and RECOMMENDS what to do. This is the absolute minimum you should expect. But it means accountability is still a bit fuzzy ("But we agreed . . .") and if they recommend something poor, you may end up by just telling them what to do (back to Level 2). But it gives a basis for some coaching (pull – of which more later).

Level 4 – the follower acts and then INFORMS IMMEDIATELY what they have done. This is more proactive but raises two issues – the first is that you are flooded with information, and second the level of confidence is not where it needs to be. It is the "Jesuit" approach – it is easier to seek forgiveness than ask permission (with apologies to any Jesuits reading this book!). It also raises the issue that there does not seem to be a stable routine for reporting.

Level 5 – the follower acts and then INFORMS ROUTINELY what they have done. This is the best level to move towards self-organisation. And you need a routine (and not one which looks like micro-managing!).

Levels of Followership		Possible response
Level 1	WAITS to be told	Ask "Why did you not come and see me?" or "Ask me next time!"
2	ASKS to be told	Say: "What would you suggest?" or "Go away and find out the options"
3	RECOMMENDS for approval	Say "Why are you asking?" or "Next time just do it and let me know!"
4	INFORMS IMMEDIATELY	Say "Why are you telling me?" or "Next time just include it in the report/meeting"
5	INFORMS ROUTINELY	Move gradually to exception reporting
6	SELF-ORGANISES	

Figure 6.1 Moving folks to Level 6 followership

Level 6 – the follower SELF-ORGANISES and only reports exceptions or when support is needed by the leader. This is the best level.

The strategy here is to identify and then nudge, step by step. One should not make the mistake of Brian, in *The Life of Brian*, who tries to get those following him to move from Level 2 to full empowerment in one go (for light relief see: https://www.youtube.com/watch?v=KHbzSif78qQ). One needs to first identify where people are and then nudge them, over time, to the next level, one level at a time.

Figure 6.1 gives some possible things to say to nudge them, one level at a time, to the next level. Each person will differ. You can see that the first two to three levels use telling – but in fact that is a "sell" in that you give the customer what they want – to be told! But you are not telling the "what" but the "how" you want the follower to operate. Some other strategies to employ with followers who do not want to respond to devolvement or self-organisation are:

1   Look at your team – "buddy up" those who do step up with those who do not and so give both a development opportunity as well as move followers along.

2   Have a "HOW" conversation and ask questions (see below for a fuller technique) such as "I have confidence in you, you are doing a great job, but I could not help noticing that you keep asking permission – why is that?". The issue could be confidence, it could be someone who has been micro-managed in the past and cannot kick the habit, or it could be the way the follower sees you and misinterprets what you want!

3   Ask if the follower is in the right place – everyone is a star but sometimes they need moving to where they can really shine.

The underlying strategy here is to enable followers to think for themselves within a good understanding of the context. A powerful approach is to use effective questioning techniques. A good roadmap for this is the GROW model.

This is a powerful questioning technique which guides the individual to think through how to solve issues and problems. There are a variety of questions one can ask. To show how powerful this approach is, here is another exercise. Pick something that you would like to achieve, that involves other people, but you are not sure how you can do it. Then ask yourself the following GROW example questions, and for each one write down the answer.

G oal

R eality

O ptions

W ill/Wrap-up

Figure 6.2 GROW

POSSIBLE QUESTIONS FOR GOAL:

> What do you want to achieve now or in the future?
> What benefits will you get?
> What is the significance of these benefits?
> What will happen if you do not achieve this?
> What is the significance of not achieving this?

POSSIBLE QUESTIONS FOR REALITY:

> What have you done to achieve the goal?
> How far away are you from the goal and what is the measure of distance?
> What has blocked you so far? How might you overcome these blockages?
> What are the constraints inside you to achieving the goal?
> Are there particular people who could help you achieve the goal? Can you visualise a person helping you?

POSSIBLE QUESTIONS FOR OPTIONS:

> What could you do to move toward this goal?
> What else could you do? Repeat, repeat . . .
> If you had a lot of time, what could you do?
> If you had no limits on resources what could you do?
> If you did nothing but just asked for help, what would be the outcome?
> Is there someone who could show you what to do?
> How does your choice help you reach the goal?

POSSIBLE QUESTIONS FOR WILL/WRAP-UP:

> How many of the options do you want to choose?
> How will you know you have reached the goal?
> Who else needs to know about the plan? How will you inform them?
> When will you take the first step? And what, specifically, will that be?

I hope the exercise was useful and of course I have no idea what goal you identified – so to coach one needs to ask questions, and you do not need to know much about the content! The approach above was linear but, in reality, one tends to jump around the

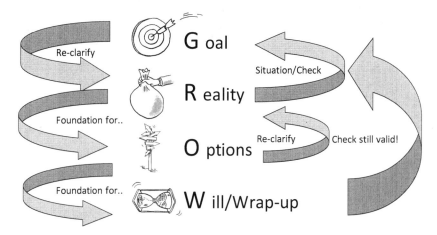

Figure 6.3 GROW dynamic

model a bit in a conversation. For example, an option could in fact highlight an underlying goal which needs to be reframed.

The questions above were open (i.e. could not be answered by yes or no, like a closed question) and non-suggestive. But the CAL approach has a few other types of questions:

- Closed and suggestive – this is for when a person has no idea! E.g.: "I found doing X, Y, Z can help – would that work for you?". Or if the person comes up with an idea which you know will cause other problems: "Do you think John in marketing will be happy with that?".
- Open and suggestive – this is to build on the closed and suggestive. If they say an idea you propose can work you could ask "Why would that work?" or "How could you make that work?" etc.
- Closed and non-suggestive – this is to use as a summary every few minutes to check your understanding and keep things on track.

A good mix is 80% open, 20% closed and 80% non-suggestive, 20% suggestive. This then is a mix of 80% pull and 20% push, and a mix of the "involve" strategy (80%) and "sell" strategy (20%) from the previous chapter.

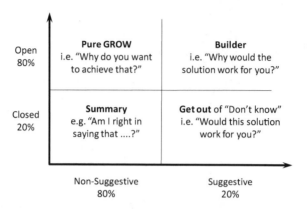

Figure 6.4 Types of questions

Using this coaching technique as a leader does take time – but it saves time overall as your team becomes more able to think things through and get on and solve problems in a fully account-able way, leaving you time both to use coaching to develop your people (playing the leadership 1.0 game in a more effective way, as well as doing leadership 2.0 and 3.0). And it gives time for you to be more strategic, get off the hamster wheel and onto the balcony to reflect more and anticipate more.

An analysis of the post-four months reports of some 700 managers who have applied the CAL approach in a mindful way shows two key benefits emerge. First, their team becomes more self-organising and works better, getter results faster for less leadership effort. Second, it saves a lot more time to do more important things by stopping doing things that are not value-adding and devolving a lot to the team. Some of the benefits reported by the 700 participants within these two themes of "team" and "time" are shown in Figure 6.5.

I can imagine that you have come up with some new thoughts:

• What are the things you should KEEP doing?
• What are the things you do not do enough of and so should INCREASE?
• What are the things you can START doing?
• What are the things you should STOP doing?

And these probably add or build on those from the other chapters – so HOW to get the changes you have identified so far actually happening?

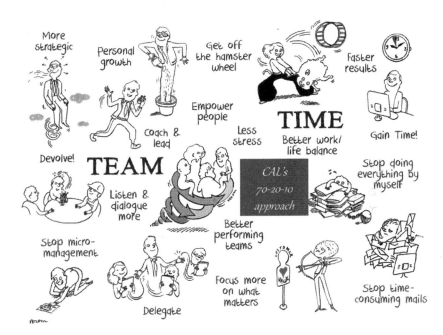

Figure 6.5 CAL Programme benefits

CHAPTER 7

HOW to make the change happen

There are two broad approaches to change. Both work, and both are needed. The first is linear and one which you are no doubt already aware of, but it is still worth looking at, not least the typical traps that you might fall into. The second approach is even more dynamic and draws on Complexity Science.

Let's look at the first one, based on my much earlier book *Practical Business Re-engineering: Tools and Techniques for Achieving Effective Change* (Obolensky, 1994).

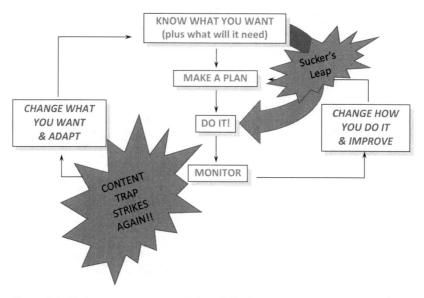

Figure 7.1 Change management 101 and the key trap

It's deceptively simple (but as Clausewitz said, "Everything in war is simple, but the simplest things are sometimes the hardest to achieve"). It's pretty linear – Know what you want, then Make a plan, then Do it and then Monitor – and if what you get is not what you want, either change the plan or change the objective. And the biggest trap is we spend all our time on the WHAT and never enough time on the HOW (aka the "Sucker's Leap" as the "Content Trap" strikes again!). However, if well done, this can get change going when things are "complicated" (not "complex" which we look at later!). Let's briefly consider each step and the questions that need to be answered, and we will assume we are talking about a large-scale organisational change (so for small individual change some questions are irrelevant):

Know what you want – this is about the WHY and the WHAT:

The WHY:

Is there a clear and shared need for change?
Benefits of achieving? Consequences of not achieving?

The WHAT:

Are all stakeholder needs addressed?
Is the strategy based on sound analysis?
Is the strategy comprehensive – external backed by internal (note: "Culture eats strategy for breakfast")?

Make a plan – this is all about the HOW:

Is there a clear programme of coordinated well-planned projects?
Is there a coordination full-time team, governance (e.g. steering group) and Change Operations Room?
Does the change programme have an identity?
Are change champions identified and mobilised?
Is there a clear engagement strategy to ensure commitment rather than just compliance?

Do it – this is about the WHO, WHEN and WHERE:

Is leadership visibly supporting the change by exemplifying changed behaviours?
Are leaders supported by leadership development?
Are change management skills being trained in to support the change programme?
Is the flexibility in place to be agile and adaptive as well as determined and focused (Yin-Yang)?
Is PULL as well as PUSH in place (Yin-Yang)?

Monitor – this is about ensuring measures are in place to see progress with good feedback:

Are soft as well as hard measures in place? (Yin-Yang)
Is there transparency so all can see progress and address barriers as they arise?
Can the top leadership see quickly how progress is going (e.g. Change Operations Centre)?
Is success celebrated widely and those involved given visible recognition?

Change the HOW or the WHAT – this is to ensure that the programme is agile and adaptive:

Is the strategy agile enough to seize new opportunities and let go of ones which do not deliver?
Are projects and programmes designed to "fail fast"?
Are pilots given enough room to succeed/gather learning?
Is there a closed feedback loop for learning and continued innovation?

The approach above is good for "complicated" change – i.e. when there is an analytical solution. But what about "complex" change where variables are so inter-connected, and the context is VUCA? For this approach we can draw on Complexity Science, and specifically the butterfly effect and phase transitions. Let's look at the butterfly effect first.

Most have heard of the butterfly effect. But not many know the full story and where it came from.

Much work was done in the 1970s when the new theories of chaos were really beginning to emerge. Strangely enough, most papers in various scientific fields began to appear independently of each other in 1970. Sadly, very few were aware that a lot of work had already been done 10 years earlier. It seemed no one thought of looking in the *Journal of Atmospheric Sciences*, volume 20, published in 1963. Over a decade before the term "chaos mathematics" was first coined, an article entitled "Deterministic Non-Periodic Flow" by Edward Lorenz described one of the most famous manifestations of chaos mathematics – the butterfly effect. Its more technical term is "Lorenz's Strange Attractor".

Edward Lorenz was a keen mathematician but, failing to get a job as a maths teacher, ended up working as a research meteorologist. He built a mini-weather system simulator on a Royal McBee computer in 1960. In the winter of 1961 he wanted to study again a weather simulation he had just spent several days running, and so typed in the starting parameters once more. These consisted of a very lengthy code of numbers, each with a long decimal point such as 0.50167507061956. The numbers represented changes in three variables of temperature, pressure and wind speed. To save time, he left the final few numbers off as this in meteorological terms was insignificant – "like a seagull fart in a hurricane" was the apparent significance he was reported to comment to a colleague.

The simulation ran at first exactly as before, but after a couple of days some very small differences occurred to the first run. After a while these differences grew to an outcome that was vastly different – the simulation ended in a weather state poles apart from the first run, despite such a very small change at the start. Lorenz made an accidental but very significant discovery – that a very small change within a complex system (such as weather) can produce a very large difference to what would have otherwise happened. In other words, when a situation has a great sensitivity to initial conditions a small change can have a disproportionate effect. When he worked out why this was, he found that even complex and chaotic systems, which are unpredictable in the long run, have an underlying pattern.

This accidental discovery was given the technical name "sensitive dependence on initial conditions". When Lorenz presented his paper several years later to the 139th meeting of the American Association for the Advancement of Science in Washington in 1972, he titled his presentation paper "Predictability: Does the flap of a butterfly's wings in Brazil set off a tornado in Texas?" (Lorenz, 1972). His answer was, predictably, ambiguous whilst focusing on the instability of the atmosphere. The Lorenz's butterfly effect can be explained by three (temperature, pressure and wind speed) simultaneous non-linear differential equations which have an infinite number of possible solutions.

The butterfly effect is very significant as, on the face of it, it seems to break the first law of thermodynamics, sometimes known as the Law of the Conservation of Energy, which can be summarised as: the effort you put in will dictate the result you get out. Yet within complex organisations, small changes can yield large results. When graphed in two dimensions (it is in fact a three-dimensional model), Lorenz's equation gives a picture, as shown in Figure 7.2, which shows why the term "butterfly effect" is used (which, I am sure you will agree, is slightly more agreeable than "the seagull fart effect"!).

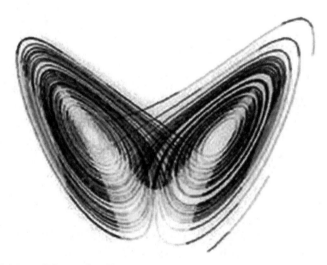

Figure 7.2 Lorenz's butterfly effect

So, what's this got to do with leadership? Wind the clock forward to 1999, and Collins wrote a great article in *Harvard Business Review* called "Turning Goals into Results: The power of catalytic mechanisms". According to Collins, such catalytic mechanisms (which we call CatMecs – small things that get big results) have five characteristics:

1   They produce results in unpredictable ways. In some ways this links to the principle of needing to have a degree of tolerance to chaos and ambiguity.
2   They distribute power, often to the discomfort of those who traditionally hold power.
3   They have teeth. Catalytic mechanisms need to be specific and cannot be half measures!
4   They help "eject viruses". A lot of controls are geared at getting people to act in a certain way, the "right way". Catalytic mechanisms help organisations get the right people in the first place.
5   They produce ongoing effects. They are not like the one-off rousing speech or motivating event. Catalytic mechanisms run themselves and produce ongoing effects.

To make them work we would add the following:

1   Create political space. There may many processes that get in the way of your team self-organising – instead of trying to change the process, talk about doing a pilot "to get better results, faster for less cost" or an experiment to innovate a new and more effective way. People hate change – especially when a process has legacy and political interest. But few people hate a pilot or experiment to get better results. Calculate the downside risk and upside potential.
2   Create space in time – as will be seen below, when we bring phase transition theory into the equation, emergence takes time. So, make sure you create the time to do the pilot and run it all the way through – it can be a bumpy ride!

So why is it sometimes a bumpy ride? Emergence occurs in bumps, not as a smooth line. To understand this, let's look at how emergence can occur. For this we can use the Complexity Science "buttons" simulation. You can see the full simulation at: https://www.youtube.com/watch?v=78Aggi4frb4 and Figure 7.3 shows the end result. In the bottom half of the figure one can see a number of "buttons" randomly spread across a table which have been joined at random by cotton "thread". The top left part of the window shows the number of buttons in the largest cluster – this obviously starts with two and then builds up as pairs of buttons are connected into larger clusters. The top-right window shows the number of buttons connected on the x axis, with the number of buttons in the largest cluster on the y axis. You will note that the graph jumps twice – each being a phase transition.

If one can imagine that the buttons are not buttons, but people within an organisation, and that the thread is not thread but random conversations, then the number of buttons in a cluster can become connected insight, and the phased transition/

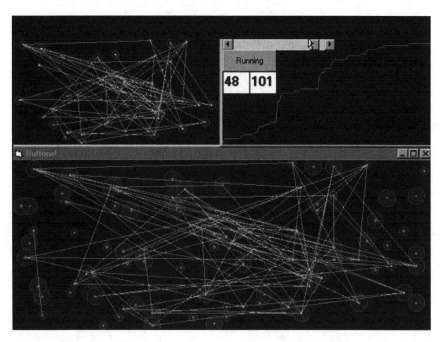

Figure 7.3 Phase transitions

bifurcation graph can illustrate the "ah-ha!" phenomenon. You have seen this yourself. You have a random conversation at the coffee machine, and then later you have a conversation on the train home with a stranger, and then you have a conversation at home and suddenly – wham! – you make a connection and get an insight. An "ah-ha" moment. This equates to a bifurcation of meaning, a phase transition from random conversations into deeper meaning. And it's the same with catalytic mechanisms when they are first put in place – things get worse, then better, then worse, then better, then worse and then – wham! – they can work . . . or not. There is no certainty, but certainly probability. That's why they need time, as well as a good intuition of something that could work. A few other points:

- The process is random and messy – but is recognisable and often called "coincidence" or "synchronicity". Synchronicity has been applied to leadership before, perhaps the best example being the seminal book by Jo Jaworski (1996), *Synchronicity: The Inner Path of Leadership*.
- A "critical mass" of randomness is needed to get meaning. This is randomness that cannot be controlled but is vital for obtaining a controlled result, paradoxical as that may sound.
- Things progress in messy steps and not in a smooth line. So, one needs to be comfortable with a messy process – this seems antithetical to most management theory. Emergence is complex – complexity is messy.

There are a few other lessons one can draw from the buttons simulation. If we see an organisation as a network of people, and that random conversations can generate meaning, we can understand why innovative companies break down functional and hierarchical silos as well as employ open space to enable random contact across boundaries. Sadly, the way we frequently organise cuts these "threads".

The chapter that follows has some examples and stories of what we have been talking about. But for now, here are some questions to consider.

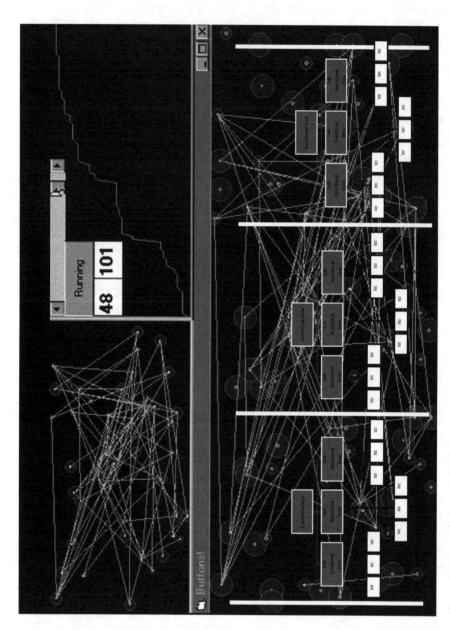

Figure 7.4 Boundaries cut the links

1   Look through the notes and KISS actions (the STARTS and STOPS) you have considered. Some may need the linear approach, but many can be implemented by doing a few small things (CatMecs). What CatMecs can you identify to try out in your day-to-day job?
2   What is getting in the way of your team being self-organised? What CatMecs can you try you to remove those barriers?

Also:

*   What are the things you should KEEP doing?
*   What are the things you do not do enough of and so should INCREASE?
*   What are the things you can START doing?
*   What are the things you should STOP doing?

So far, we have shared some new ways of looking at things, as well as challenged you with many questions to consider. We have not shared examples or stories as we wanted you to be focused on you, not others! But examples and stories help, and so the next chapter has a few to provide further inspiration.

References

Collins, J. (1999), "Turning Goals into Results: The Power of Catalytic Mechanisms", *Harvard Business Review*, July–August.
Jaworski, J. (1996), *Synchronicity – The Inner Path of Leadership*, San Francisco: Berrett-Koehler.
Lorenz, E. (1963), "Deterministic Non-periodic Flow", *Journal of Atmospheric Sciences* 20, 130–141.
Lorenz, E (1972) "Predictability: Does the flap of a butterfly's wing s in Brazil set off a tornado in Texas?", paper presented before the American Association for the Advancement of Science, December 29.
Obolensky, N. (1994), *Practical Business Re-engineering: Tools and Techniques for Achieving Effective Change*, London: Kogan Page.

8 *A few examples and brief stories*

There are lot of stories and case studies which exemplify what we have been talking about. Below are but a few. However, the best story is the one you craft for yourself, although you may get some inspiration from others.

Examples of CatMecs and randomness – some company examples

- The story of solving random faults randomly and Xerox. You may not remember, but when photocopiers first hit the scene they had an annoying habit of breaking down but then working again. To counter this, Xerox would employ teams of engineers in vans to react quickly to fix the problem, being tasked by a one-way radio system to the client who would call in with the problem. More often than not, by the time the engineer turned up, the fault had vanished. Xerox called in a range of experts, including a team from the Santa Fe Institute (set up for Complexity Science research). It was suggested that the van drivers be given two-way radios. Soon the drivers were using the radios for random conversation – and the effectiveness of repairing ghost faults rose by 80 per cent in all areas except one. The exception to the improvement was the area where the manager of the team heard them having random conversations, and so told them to stop. In that case it was clear that the critical mass "tipping point" was never achieved.

- The story of enabling random conversations and Symantec.
  Hal was studying for his part-time MBA and ran a technical call centre of 300 technicians covering the market in
  Europe, Middle East and Africa. The call centre provided
  technical support for users of software sold by the company.
  It was during his MBA that he first saw "buttons" simulation
  and was exposed to chaos theory. And it was then that he
  finally, in a great "ah-Ha" moment, realised why smokers
  in his call centre were more productive. He found out that
  his smokers were more productive in the first place due to
  a detailed productivity improvement study recently com-
  pleted. The call centre was facing closure with operations
  moved to India, unless productivity could be improved. Hal
  had done a very deterministic re-engineering programme,
  helped by experienced productivity consultants who had
  done things like reposition the coffee machines around the
  call centre to cut down on the walking-to-and-from time
  etc. This and other measures had seen productivity increase
  around 5% but that was not enough. One of the facts that
  came out of the research done in the productivity improvement study was that smokers in his call centre were more
  productive. He could not work out why this was – until he
  saw the buttons simulation. Then he realised that smokers would, at random, get up and go outside to smoke and
  whilst they did they had random conversations. Whilst
  doing this they gained knowledge from each other to solve
  issues in new ways, which enabled them to handle more
  calls faster. This is like the Xerox experience. Hal realised
  then that he needed a place where people could, at random,
  gather to have "smoke" breaks. So, he introduced one small
  change and waited to see what would happen. He created a
  space where people could have a break and moved all the
  coffee machines into it. He put bean bags in the space as
  well. The results, which are astonishing, are shown in Figure
  8.1, with productivity measure shown by the time spent by
  callers waiting to get through (the lower the number, the
  lower the wait time and thus the higher the productivity).

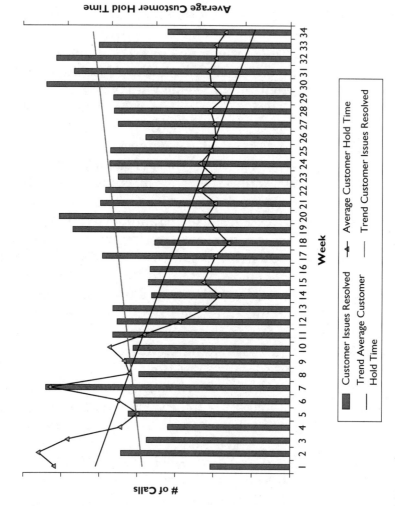

Figure 8.1 A CatMec result

This research was part of Hal's MBA and, as such, these figures and the causes for them were subject to academic scrutiny. Numbers have been withheld due to commercial sensitivity.

The first thing Hal did was to check with his line manager that he could have the space to experiment for three months. You can imagine what happened after the second week – the manager said "What's going on? You've gone against some of the consultants' recommendations!" – Hal politely informed the manager he had allowed three months to try things out. Things got better over the next few weeks to which the manager said: "It will never last – we've seen the research – repaint the factory and productivity improves but in never lasts – this is a flash in the pan!". And when things returned to where they were in week 7 the reaction was – "See! Told you so! End the pilot!" – but Hal, who understood phase transition theory, persisted. By the time the pilot ended in week 12 the results were good enough for the centre to be saved, and the improvement continued for the next couple of weeks before settling down.

- The story of self-management of random expenses and the power of transparency at Roche[1]. Managing travel out-of-pocket expenses in a large organisation is not easy, mainly because they occur due to changing circumstances and the need to spend money to get the job done is somewhat last minute. Although some expenses can be budgeted, many cannot due to the fact is impossible to predict what changing circumstance will occur. In one area of a large multinational pharma firm, Roche, a group decided to do an experiment. Like in most big companies, travel and expenses were subject to a bureaucratic process for sign-offs. This caused some frustration: "I'm responsible for €60 million in sales but need approval to buy a €3 cup of coffee", summed up the general mood. Against a pair of control groups to measure, they set up two pilot groups. These pilot groups could self-authorise their expenses, instead of going through the process of getting sign-offs for expenses. A few simple rules were re-enforced (e.g. travel as per policy, booking via the Travel Department etc). In one pilot group those who self authorised had to publish what they had spent on, and why, on a web page on the company intranet with full transparency. Another pilot group had to send their expenses by email, where slightly aggregated information would be visible to participants and line managers, but not to others.

The pilot looked to measure three things: 1) Would people become more motivated? 2) Was the new process more efficient? 3) What would happen to costs? To prevent the "Hawthorne effect" (where people change behaviour when they know they are being watched), the pilots were introduced with the minimum of fuss and in a very low-key way. Both pilot groups reported an increase in motivation, and overwhelming said the new process was better attuned to the company values and was more efficient. As for costs, the costs went down in both pilots, dramatically so in the pilot, with full transparency. The new process was not adopted widely however – perhaps indicating that unless these pilots have some form of higher sponsorship, entropy, politics and inertia can trump innovation!

Some shorter examples of self-organisation in action

- Revco Drugstores achieved a 34% increase in productivity by moving its warehouse picking from a centrally controlled to a self-organising system. It can be proven mathematically that workers spontaneously gravitate towards the most optimum way of working.
- General Motors saved $1.5 million a year by scrapping the centrally controlled paint spraying approach of trucks that came off the line at its operation at Fort Wayne. This system, which was normally controlled centrally, was replaced by a bidding system for the ten painting booths which was far more efficient. The bidding system is based on a single simple objective (paint as many trucks as possible) and a few simple rules (e.g. use as little paint as possible, if there is a long queue in front of the booth – bid zero etc.).

- In *John Deere Runs on Chaos*, Paul Roberts (2010) describes how the world's largest machinery manufacturer put complexity and chaos theory into use through a project called Vision XXI. This involved enabling a wider viewpoint for all employees (so each understood the whole rather than just their part), ensuring information flowed at all levels, and freedom of action for employees to get things done and solve problems. In many ways the John Deere story also resembles some of the principles of a fractal self-organising approach.
- And yet more: Nucor (America's most profitable steel maker), Morning Star (the world's largest tomato processor), W.L. Gore (a $3 billion high-tech company famous for its Gore-Tex fabrics), Svenska Handelsbanken (a Stockholm-based bank with more than 800 branches across Northern Europe and the UK), Sun Hydraulics (a class-leading manufacturer of hydraulic components), Valve (a pioneering developer of online games) and General Electric's jet engine plant in Durham, North Carolina, use elements of self-organisation. Thus, the average span of control in these and other vanguard organisations is more than double the US average. General Electric's Durham plant, to take a dramatic example, employs more than 300 technicians and a single supervisor: the plant manager. The facility is more than twice as productive as its sister plants in GE Aviation.

Examples of letting go and devolving more

- Mike McCormack is a senior manager with Nokia in the USA with 30 years' experience. He applied, and continues to apply some years later whilst still learning, the CAL approach after doing one of our 70-20-10 programmes. He realised he was micro-managing so stepped back more and enabled his team to come up with solutions:

  "I've made a significant impact on my direct reports and their productivity reflects it. The 70-20-10 approach has influenced my teams on a daily basis and we have savings and cost reductions as a result. The IPAS system created a discipline reflection schedule and goal-oriented plan. I've never experienced a program that continues to impact my life years after."

- Chris Cook, another senior manager in Singapore responsible for bid management in APAC, also learnt to devolve more and stopped trying to keep on top of everything:

  "I was beginning to be challenged leading a large team which was facing increasingly volatile and uncertain times. I was struggling, getting involved in everything. I was burning out. CAL opened my eyes to other leadership techniques and by applying the approach I am getting great results but for a lot less stress. I have learned how to let go and "get onto the balcony" and spend more time looking long term, whilst enabling my team to get on and achieve the day-to-day results. I am spending more time coaching and enabling, and being more strategic in my work. The extra strategic projects I'm involved in are now bringing additional financial benefits."

- And for those who like to manage using 1.0 KPIs and targets: Wells Fargo, one of USA biggest banks, dropped sales targets for sales people when it was discovered over 2 million bogus accounts were created, with over 500 employees sacked for the practice which spread back over four years. Manage to the metric, hit the target or else – this was about as much a 1.0 approach and culture as anything else. A classic case of using out-of-date deterministic methods to chase the illusion of control in a non-deterministic VUCA world!

More testimonies can be seen on our website: www.Complex AdaptiveLeadership.com

Examples of employing the butterfly effect/catalytic mechanisms

- Granite Rock wanted to be the market leader in customer service. They decided to allow customers to "short pay".

At the bottom of each invoice one can find the following: "If you are not satisfied for any reason, don't pay us for it. Simply scratch out the line item, write a brief note about the problem, and return a copy of this invoice along with your check for the balance". Over the years this small addition to the invoice has had a profoundly positive impact.

- Mike Jackson, then CEO of financial services company Birmingham Midshires in the UK, included his personal phone number on complaint forms. These forms stated if the complaints were not dealt with in a quick and polite way, the customer could phone him personally. The company was struggling to survive, and it identified customer service as a critical opportunity. The actual number of calls the CEO received was negligible but such a small change had a large and beneficial effect on staff handling complaints, as well as on customer perceptions. The company's poor situation was turned around and it became an award winner for customer service. Again, this initiative was but one of a variety of efforts taken and shows how a relatively simple thing can help achieve a larger effect.

- Bill Gore, founder of W.L. Gore & Associates, wanted the company to have a "natural leadership" style (similar to 4.0). So, they have a policy which allows staff to "sack" their bosses. They cannot sack them from the company, but if they feel their boss is not providing the right support, they can simply bypass them and choose another person to report to.

- National Vulcan (an engineering insurance company), in order to enable a more team-based self-organising culture, removed without warning the time punch machines used by staff to clock in. This small move had a huge effect on changing the culture in the desired direction.

- 3M has a strong commitment to innovation, aiming to have 25% of revenue from products less than five years old. To support this, they have the policy of "bootleg time" which allows each employee 15% of his time and available resources to be devoted to pet projects. Staff are encouraged to take the lead and define new products – the most well-known which resulted from this was the Post-it™ note.

Example of using fractal pattern recognition

• The US retailer Target's Big Data analysis of its premium card holders shows similar patterns to Mandelbrot's set: there are vast periods of time when the shoppers buy the same things, at more or less the same rate and at the same time. There are few to no changes and it is very difficult to motivate the shopper to change. However, Target's analysis also showed that there are periods in their premium card-holders' life when they change buying patterns and the most marked period occurs before and after having a baby. Therefore, the transition period between no child and child (i.e. pregnancy) becomes an incredibly important and interesting boundary condition – because during this time, you can influence the shopper to change his/her shopping patterns and this new pattern will last a very long time. This insight led Target to dive deeper into their shoppers' buying patterns during pregnancy and to analyse in-depth what they bought and when. They became so good at understanding the buying patterns of "pregnant households" that they can identify the baby's due date to within three weeks.

   Target's analysis is similar to deep diving the Mandelbrot set; the deeper you go, the more interesting it becomes. I guess the major difference is that Mandelbrot dives result in pleasing aesthetics while the Target dives generate pleasing bottom lines. However, "Big Data" can have a double edge – Target suffered due to the recent hack of their consumer database that harvested about 40 million debit and credit card numbers as well as personal information for another 70 million people. The hack occurred through a single email sent to a small air-conditioning repair and maintenance shop in Sharpsburg, Pennsylvania, called Fazio Mechanical Services, which had a supplier contract with the local Target store and was therefore linked into their system. This is also a story of the butterfly effect – i.e. a tiny, incremental event causing a huge effect. It was through this tiny hole, way off in a corner of the system, that the hackers gained access to the complete database. This hack has had a huge, negative impact on Target's brand image and bottom line. "Big Data" may be fractal and an opportunity, but it can have big risks too![2]

Notes

1 My thanks to Professor Julian Birkinshaw at London Business School and Kristen Pressner at Roche for providing this example.
2 My thanks to Doug Dean, a CAL Associate, for providing the story of Target.

Reference

Roberts, P. (2010), *John Deere Runs on Chaos*, Edition 19, London: Fast Company.

9 *So what now?*

Let's summarise briefly the journey so far. You've read the book and now understand the following key points:

- The context of leadership has changed faster than our assumption of what it is, and we need to complement and enable the thousands-of-years old leadership 1.0 approach with 2.0 (sideways and outwards) and 3.0 (upwards) into a dynamic of leadership 4.0 – a complex dynamic.
- Three states typically co-exist – the "simple" (which needs categorisation and process), the "complicated" (which needs analysis and traditional decision-making) and the "complex" (which needs dynamic probing with feedback loops).
- Complexity Science shows that complex dynamics and systems mostly have inherent self-organisation following a few simple rules which enable emergence.
- Eight key principles need to be in place for self-organisation to emerge, but this needs leaders to have a 4.0 mindset to release fully the potential and enable such agility.
- Four key strategies need to be employed in a dynamic mix of "push" and "pull" by leaders, when to get a grip and when to let go. The hardest one is to know when and how to let go, step back and allow flow.
- Using deterministic approaches, and being addicted to action and urgency, can lead to spending time in delusion – a waste of salary!

- Followers need to be nudged along to accept more responsibility and accountability, and each person will differ and start at a different level.
- To enable change to occur two broad approaches need to be implemented – complicated change needs a linear approach with a feedback loop (note: the content trap!) and this can be complemented for complex change using CatMecs (note: phase transitions!)
- Various examples and stories are out there – but the best story is the one you craft for yourself!

So, what now? If you want to follow this journey, this book is just a start – but reflective practice and application is where the payback rests. Why reflective practice? We so easily get caught on the hamster wheel – our experience, beliefs, insights as well as demands on our time lead us to decide then act immediately, and we quickly get caught up endlessly going round and round.

The only way I know to get out of this cycle, and jump off that wheel and onto the balcony, is to STOP – THINK – REFLECT – LOG, with reflection being the key part.

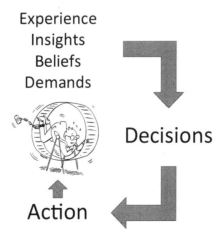

Figure 9.1 Caught on the hamster wheel

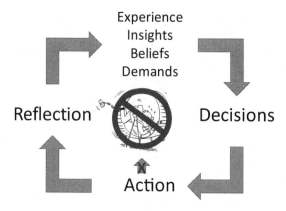

Experience
Insights
Beliefs
Demands

Reflection   Decisions

Action

Figure 9.2 Reflection – jumping off the hamster wheel

A key part of this is to keep a diary or a log of your reflections as a habit. This enables you to see how you progress on the journey, and this allows issues and potential to emerge over time. Keeping a diary or a log may seem a little quaint and old-fashioned, but there is a large amount of different research which shows that leaders who do this in today's busy, busy world perform better than others. There are also other benefits which can accrue.

LEARNING BY THINKING:
OVERCOMING THE BIAS FOR ACTION THROUGH REFLECTION

- Enhances performance and career success
- Improves focus
- Increases patience
- Enables better planning
- Assists personal growth
- Helps create self-awareness

≡   FSTCOMPANY

2 MINUTE READ | LEADERSHIP

Why You Should Keep A Journal At Work

Dust off the diary from your teenage years. A 15-minute writing exercise at the end of your workday can make you more successful.

Figure 9.3 Benefits of logging reflections

So here is the next exercise:

1   Go back and look at the answers to the questions in this book at the end of each chapter – you might want to revisit them!
2   Get a notebook or diary – call it something – names like "Getting off the hamster wheel", "More for less", "Self-organised self-organisation" works for some – you may have a better idea.
3   At the front, write down the key things you would like to implement from your KISSes – especially the starts and most important the STOPS!
4   Each day spend five minutes noting down your answers to the following three questions:

   a   Score out of 10 (10 being highest) – "What impact did I have today?"
   b   Answer – "What went well?"
   c   Answer – "What needs more focus?"

5   Each week – look at the busy, busy week ahead and write down how you can play the game differently, getting 4.0 well established – be patient, it takes time!
6   Each month – look back at what you have written and reflect:

   a   What seems to be emerging which needs attention?
   b   What other KISSes are needed?

7   Try to find another person on the journey to discuss and support/challenge and co-coach

The journey for you has just begun. And, learning from many others who have set off before you, after four months (or even sooner!) you should start to see some real differences and begin to get better results, faster and for less effort . . .

You can catch up on news, and any new ideas which emerge, at: www.ComplexAdaptiveLeadership.com

Want to share learning and insights with other readers? A group is available at: https://www.linkedin.com/groups/4328394

And meanwhile, I wish you the very best!

Index

Page numbers in *italics* refer to figures.